*Through the Years*

(ON THE BACK COVER, CENTER) Stanley and Lillian Benjamin with their dog, Peeky, at the Little Pink House in Indian River, Michigan, shortly after Stanley's retirement from Galesburg, Michigan, 1962.

# Through the Years

**THE POEMS OF**
*Rev. Stanley L. Benjamin*
(A POET OF THE NORTHWOODS)

Revised Edition
Edited and with a new introduction by
*Stanley G. Benjamin,*
*Amanda J. Holmes &*
*Daniel W. Stewart*

First edition copyright © 1971 by Stanley L. Benjamin.
New introduction copyright © 2022 by Stanley G. Benjamin.
All rights reserved.

Production of this revised and expanded edition of *Through the Years* has been a team and family effort, with special contributions from Stanley G. Benjamin, Amanda J. Holmes, and Daniel W. Stewart.

This volume contains the poems from the original volume, as well as some additional poems also composed by Stanley L. Benjamin that had been collected among the family. We have tried to incorporate a few corrections and changes the author made by hand in the published original. We have attempted as much as possible to preserve the order of the original version but some variation has been unavoidable. Behind all of the changes is our attempt to preserve not only the poems but also the intent of the author.

ISBN (hardcover): 978-1-949285-05-5
ISBN (softcover): 978-1-949285-06-2

PUBLISHED BY
Daniel W. Stewart
P.O. Box 137
Omena, Michigan 49674

# Table of Contents

The Stan & Lillian Tree:
*An Introduction to the Updated Edition by Stanley G. Benjamin* . xi
Where Stan & Lillian Lived . . . . . . . . . . . . xv
"Mending Soles and Souls, Stanley Benjamin Works His Way Through College," from *The Albion Recorder* (1924) . . . . xvi
About the Author . . . . . . . . . . . . . . . xix
Introduction (1971) . . . . . . . . . . . . . xlvi

PART 1
## JUST FOR THE KIDS

String Bean . . . . . . . . . . . . . . . . 3
Granddaughter Number 2 . . . . . . . . . . . 4
To the First Grandson . . . . . . . . . . . . 6
To Stan . . . . . . . . . . . . . . . . . 10
Claudia Cade . . . . . . . . . . . . . . . 11
Jennifer Ruth . . . . . . . . . . . . . . . 12
Richard John . . . . . . . . . . . . . . . 13
"K" . . . . . . . . . . . . . . . . . . 15
Number 15 . . . . . . . . . . . . . . . . 16
Two Yards . . . . . . . . . . . . . . . . 17
Rocket Trip . . . . . . . . . . . . . . . . 18
Carrots . . . . . . . . . . . . . . . . . 19
Pretty Little Pussy Cat . . . . . . . . . . . . 20
Passing Years . . . . . . . . . . . . . . . 21
The Potato . . . . . . . . . . . . . . . . 22

PART 2
## LET'S GO FISHING

Trout Fever . . . . . . . . . . . . . . . . 27
Biology . . . . . . . . . . . . . . . . . 29
Lone Fisherman . . . . . . . . . . . . . . 31
Angler's Tragedy . . . . . . . . . . . . . . 33
Big Trout from a Tiny Stream . . . . . . . . . . 34
The One That Got Away . . . . . . . . . . . 36

PART 3
## *NATURE*

| | |
|---|---|
| Farewell to the Forest | 38 |
| "Timber" | 41 |
| Deer Season | 42 |
| Forest Trail | 45 |
| To a Trailing Arbutus | 46 |
| Hill Folks and Plains People | 48 |
| Alone | 50 |
| Storm Over Lake Louise | 51 |
| Evening on Lake Louise | 52 |
| October | 53 |
| Trailing Arbutus | 54 |
| Bay-View Sunset | 55 |
| Ten Sounds I Love to Hear | 56 |
| Two Months | 57 |
| Winter Nights | 58 |

PART 4
## *A BIT OF NONSENSE NOW AND THEN*

| | |
|---|---|
| The Evolution of a Golfer | 84 |
| Opportunity Knocks but once | 88 |
| Tragedy at the Zoo | 89 |
| *Anopheles Quadrimaculatus* | 90 |
| A Song of Two Sea-Gulls | 92 |
| Advice to a Young Man | 94 |
| Freedom | 96 |
| Women's Uplift Club | 98 |
| Yust a Yoke | 99 |
| The Fly | 100 |

PART 5
## *HISTORY—AND THE WAR YEARS*

| | |
|---|---|
| War-Time Rationing | 01, |
| We'll Be Seeing More of You | 102 |
| Wings in the Sky | 103 |
| William Tuffs | 104 |

| | |
|---|---|
| Wahbememe | .106 |
| To Wahbememe (a sequel) | .110 |
| Jud Sepsey | .111 |
| War Memories | .112 |
| Conflict | .114 |
| The Times Have Changed | .116 |
| They March Past Singing | .119 |

PART 6
## ROMANCE

| | |
|---|---|
| First Love | .122 |
| Dungeon | .123 |
| Parallel Lines | .124 |
| Corn | .125 |
| Evening on the Lake | .126 |
| Snow | .127 |
| Jealousy | .128 |
| Timid Lover | .129 |
| Silver Wedding | .130 |
| Kinds of Love | .132 |
| Hopeless Lover | .133 |
| Generation Gap | .134 |

PART 7
## PEOPLE AND PLACES

| | |
|---|---|
| Fate Rides the Evening Mail | .142 |
| To a Gray Hair | .149 |
| Alas! Atlas | .150 |
| Independence | .152 |
| Two Views of life | .153 |
| Hope | .154 |
| Whistle | .155 |
| Ants | .156 |
| April Snow | .157 |
| Spinster's Soliloquy | .158 |
| I Race the Years | .159 |
| Snow at Night | .160 |

| | |
|---|---|
| Little Jim Horner | 161 |
| Lines to a Very Recent Father | 162 |
| Life | 163 |
| I Walk Life's Path | 164 |
| A Song of Revolt | 165 |
| Anticipation and Reality | 166 |
| From the Blue-Water Bridge | 168 |
| Deserted House | 170 |
| Cottage in Winter | 172 |
| Spring | 173 |
| The Teacher | 174 |

PART 8
## RELIGION

| | |
|---|---|
| Two Prayers | 180 |
| Failure | 182 |
| Creation | 183 |
| Squire Burger | 184 |
| Spring Meditation | 186 |
| Life's Challenge | 187 |
| A Prayer | 188 |
| Easter | 189 |
| Not My Hands | 190 |
| A Wish and a Prayer | 193 |
| There Were Ten: A Story for Thanksgiving | 194 |
| Life Values | 196 |
| To Myself at 70 | 197 |
| New Years Audit | 198 |
| My Neighbor | 200 |
| City of Sand | 202 |
| Another Valley | 204 |

Poetry is an attempt to imprison laughter, understanding, beauty, love and faith in a cage of words. The attempt is never fully successful; but the poet must keep on trying.

*–Stanley L. Benjamin, 1971*

Stanley and Lillian Benjamin show their adventurous spirits on a visit to Great Falls, Virginia, 6 April 1953.

## THE STAN & LILLIAN TREE

An Introduction to the Updated, Illustrated Edition by
**Stanley G. Benjamin**, grandson to Stanley L. Benjamin

HIGHWAYS ARE A GOOD PLACE TO HAVE TO MULL OVER WHERE WE'VE come from and where we're going. In 1999, my dad (Uncle Bob to my cousins), my brother Bruce and I were on the Pennsylvania Turnpike, heading back eastward from Wisconsin and Michigan after a gala Benjamin reunion of Grandpa Stan's and Grandma Lillian's descendants (including a celebration of 50-year anniversaries for aunts and uncles). I had been out of touch with my cousins for most of the previous 20 years due to absorption with my own life in Pennsylvania and Colorado. Bruce was driving in the front seat of the car with Dad, then 77; behind them, I quietly wondered: Who were these people we had just seen and chatted with and heard about, this vast tribe of Benjamins? And how had my DNA and character evolved from them?

For all of us from the Stan & Lillian tree, Grandpa's book of poetry, *Through the Years*, self-published in 1971, was a marvelous gift: it revealed what he cared about most in the world around him, and he had fun doing it. He added a small autobiography entitled "About the Author." Grandpa wrote this book to introduce his poems. Now, we "grandkids" republish it to introduce him, along with Grandma, their own upbringings, and their lives together from which a tree sprung of which we are branches.

Grandpa Stan, born in 1895 in St. Joseph County in southwestern Michigan, was the second of three brothers, with his older brother, John S. Benjamin (who went by his middle name, Serell), and his younger brother, Stilwell. Their parents, William Henry Benjamin and Cora Belle Langton Benjamin, were both born also in rural southwestern Michigan (William in 1866, Cora Belle one year later). Great-Grandma Cora Belle's parents had emigrated to the U.S. from England. Great-Grandpa Will taught in a one-room schoolhouse, like those that both of them had attended in the 1870s. Their house had a substantial book collection. Great-Grandma Cora Belle suddenly died at home at the age of only 39 when Grandpa was only 12. After Grandpa Stan's high-school graduation in Constantine in 1913 and a fire that had destroyed their house including the library, Great-Grandpa Will and the three sons moved to Emmet County in northern

Michigan. There, Great-Grandpa Will remarried to Rena Wilson, with whom he had four daughters, Mary, Ruth, Maude and Hilda, Grandpa Stan's half-sisters. These four daughters were an important part of the extended Stan & Lillian family in later years. Letters to Hilda show that Great-Grandpa Will Benjamin was certainly trained well with beautiful florid handwriting style, and Hilda reported that her father was a quiet man with great kindness.

Grandma Lillian, born in 1897 up north in Harbor Springs, Michigan, also in Emmet County, was the fourth of five siblings. Her parents, Edward Couch (who grew up in Ontario) and Hattie Griffin Couch (who grew up in New York) were married at Torch Lake in Michigan in 1880, then 27 and 17. Grandma Lillian had three older siblings, Abbie, Ray, and Velma, all more than 10 years older than her, and one younger brother, Alfred. Her family life was troubled. Their family lived in a rural area north of Boyne City, Michigan. When Lillian was about eight years old, her mother's mental illness was such that Lillian began to live with her 19-year-old sister, Velma, and Velma's husband, Bert Fetters, in Harbor Springs. Despite this difficulty and with apparently tremendous help from her sister, Lillian graduated from high school. She worked briefly at a factory in Lansing after graduation.

Grandpa Stan and Grandma Lillian met in Harbor Springs (possibly at a dance), and Grandpa returned from Army service on leave allowing them to marry in August 1918. Early pictures and poems suggest substantial mutual smittenness. The state of their lives together is described first-person by Grandpa in "About the Author." Grandpa and Grandma thrived in Albion starting in 1920 while he attended Albion College and where their sons, Bob and Ed, were born. Due to a serious family financial problem described in "About the Author," Grandpa went into a career in education at that point instead of the ministry as he had hoped for. During the next 10 years with Grandpa's first education posts in Carsonville and South Rockwood, four more kids arrived—Dot, Norma, Helen, and Bill. Then, the family of six spent the core part of their family life in Croswell, a town in the Thumb, ten miles from Lake Huron, over a 13-year period from 1934-1947.

Grandma and Grandpa found a way to have an engaging family life with their full house despite a scarcity of money. Grandma did everything at home (per Norma, the last surviving of the six children)! She was a very good cook, stretching small amounts of food to feed a family of eight. She encouraged her kids in their interests and talents (e.g., reserving a small kitchen drawer for Bob's art supplies). Grandma took the lead also with laundry, an enormous task in any era but especially before washers, but with help from Grandpa. Grandma organized the kids to household cleaning tasks—"you didn't say 'no' to her." In Croswell, kids took weekly showers at the high school, embarrassing but that was what they had.

At their houses (four of them over the twelve years in Croswell), they had a bare minimum of furniture—only three or four rocking chairs so everyone else just sat on the floor, a single ceiling light fixture, no rugs, one radio. After the dishes were done, they had a game called "dish time" in which Grandpa would ask geography questions such as what states were east or west of the Mississippi River, what states bordered other states, etc.

Norma reported that the family was a happy crew. Expectations were very high for school—reported by all six kids without exception. Norma also reported that her mother had a temper, rarely used but one to avoid if at all possible. Bob reported disappointing his father greatly by forgetting lines in a junior high play. To get out of the house, Grandma led frequent family walks around Croswell, and they even occasionally rode bikes to Lake Huron. The family drove both in summer and even winter to northern Michigan to see Great-Grandma Rena, then a widow, and Grandpa Stan's four half-sisters. Ruth and Mary both spent a year during their high school years in Croswell to help with the kids, and Maude and Hilda were like additional sisters.

Grandpa taught math in Croswell but above all, served as superintendent of the school district there. His contract was terminated in 1947 after he refused to change a grade for a football star. Their departure was abrupt—Grandma reported that he came home and said simply, "We're moving." Most of the grandkids were born and perhaps many of the poems were written during the 1947-1959 period when Grandma and Grandpa lived in Galesburg.

Northern Michigan never stopped whispering to them through their decades in southern Michigan. So they moved up to Indian River in 1959. The Indian River-Cheboygan 20-year period over the rest of their lives together is the one that we cousins remember best, including fried trout, Scrabble (Grandpa would frequently score over 300), evening drives to look for deer, more poetry writing ("To Myself at Seventy," etc.), golf and fishing, Grandma painting, Grandpa giving sermons, Grandma in the choir, and always a welcome to breakfast. Bacon was fried, kitchen sinks were regularly clogged with grease (reported by Bill), and blueberry pancakes were served, sometimes with corn. The parsonage in Cheboygan where they lived for 9 years was particularly fun to explore as a grandkid, including a not-easily-found second stairwell that opened directly into the kitchen.

Some of the recounting about them that we grandkids have heard also remind us of their humanity and ours—sometimes an "extra serving" of self-regard in Grandpa and a strong fear of aloneness in Grandma. We sometimes also find these character traits in ourselves—I do. But Grandpa was also the person who lost the longest-held position of his life because of his integrity. And how did Grandma evolve from such a traumatic childhood to make such a supportive and creative home atmosphere for six kids? They bestowed much affection on their kids and their grandchildren. They prayed for us, they kindly directed us, and they even took another role together at the church in Cheboygan to encourage community people to live lives following Christ—Grandpa was the minister for those nine years. Grandpa had a remarkable gift for expression with words, drawing from his heart to weave creative stories for us (read *Passing Years*). They were always cheering for us. Grandpa's book of poetry still speaks perhaps more loudly now than in 1971, including that encouragement for us and sense of wonder at life.

## *WHERE STAN & LILLIAN LIVED*

**Stanley Langton Benjamin** (September 19, 1895–September 28, 1979)
**Lillian Mildred Couch** (December 4, 1897–February 1, 1989)

| Place | Children Born | Graduations |
|---|---|---|
| Harbor Springs, MI (1918-1920)* | | |
| Albion, MI (1920-1924) | Bob (1921)<br>Ed (1923) | |
| Carsonville, MI (1924-1928) | Dot (1925)<br>Norma (1926) | |
| South Rockwood, MI (1928-1934) | Helen (1928)<br>Bill (1931) | |
| Croswell, MI (1934-1947) | | Bob (1938)<br>Ed (1940)<br>Dot (1942)<br>Norma (1944)<br>Helen (1946) |
| Galesburg, MI (1947-1959) | | Bill (1949) |
| Indian River, MI (1959-1962) | | |
| Cheboygan, MI (1962-1971) | | |
| Indian River, MI (1971-1979) | | |
| Sebring, FL (1972-1978, WINTERS ONLY) | | |

*After Stanley's death in 1979, Lillian lived first in Cadillac, MI, and then in Grand Rapids, MI, until her death in 1989.*

---

\*   Little Rock, AR (U.S. Army) for part of this period.

Excerpted from *The Albion Recorder*, July 19, 1924

## Mending Soles and Souls, Stanley Benjamin Works His Way Through College

Stanley Benjamin, the Petoskey young man who tapped shoes on weekdays and "sky-piloted"[*] on Sundays to put himself through Albion College, meantime supporting a wife and two children and making a record as an "all-A" student that has seldom been equaled here, has left with his little family for northern Michigan for the first vacation that he has had in the past four years. In September, Mr. Benjamin will take up his duties as superintendent of the schools at Carsonville, thriving Thumb town.

Living on a little farm near Petoskey,[†] Benjamin planned about eleven years ago to go to college and at the same time to take with him his intended bride. The war changed all that. The young man early felt the call to service for democracy and enlisted before the United States got into the war. He served for two years in camps here but did not get the opportunity to go overseas. He rose to be a lieutenant.

The close of the world conflict gave the Petoskey lad his deferred chance for both matrimony and a college career.[‡] He came to Albion in the fall of 1919 with his bride and settled down for the long grid that was to bring him his coveted Bachelor of Arts degree. Not ashamed to tackle hard work, the young man secured a position with Hahn Brothers and began to help fill the local "shoe hospital" with soles in need of repair. The figure of Benjamin, a lithe, alert chap, on his bicycle, riding around the city, ringing doorbells in search of ailing shoes became familiar around the town and his friendly but quiet ways soon brought him a steady flow of business. For four years, summer and winter, through the college year and on through the long vacation, Benjamin kept at his shoe gathering and his shoe repairing, as he prided himself on taking care of his own customers. That he made good at his task is evidenced by the words of George Hahn, one of the proprietors, "You can't say too much for that young man."

Work day and night, six days a week was not enough for the ambitious northern Michigan student to whom a college education was the biggest thing in life and worth every handicap to achieve. Young Benjamin made up his mind to preach on Sundays and thus help out the family income. With an earnest religious nature, free from sensationalism and overpretension, Benjamin knocked on the door of the First Methodist church for a "local preacher's license." The pastor of the church, Dr. W. W. Diehl, with a big heart for the sacrificing students on "college hill," backed the young man and he was given the license. It was then a

---

[*] A clergyman, and in particular a military chaplain.
[†] In Springvale, Michigan, near Boyne Falls.
[‡] At his graduation from Albion College, eleven years after graduating from high school in Constantine in 1913, Stanley was 28 years old.

short step to taking "supply work" at neighboring churches that were unable to maintain a permanent pastor. So well did young Benjamin do his preaching and so well did he gain the respect of his parishioners that for the last two years of his college course, he was the regularly appointed pastor of the Methodist church at Spring Arbor. His district superintendent, Dr. F. H. Clapp, says that he never had a better student pastor.

The biggest thing about Benjamin's success is that he more than "made good" as a student. In fact, his record for scholarship was not equaled by any young man of this year's graduating class, no matter what freedom for scholastic work others had. When class honors were announced by Dr F. S. Goodrich, acting president, at the Commencement, Stanley Benjamin was one of the two seniors to be granted "highest honors," the other being Miss Norma Sleight of this city. To attain this honor Benjamin had to have a record of no grade below B during his entire course of four years. Dr. A. H. Harrop, professor of Latin and Greek languages and literature, states that Benjamin is one of the most brilliant students that has ever taken his courses.

Albion people say that Mr. Benjamin has earned his vacation. With no financial help from anyone, he has given himself an education, kept his family of wife, and two children, and paid all bills as he went along, won the highest scholastic honors of the college and finished his four years with a checking account at the bank still available.

On the back of the photo is written: "Mr. Benjamin in Old School he attended near Constantine, Michigan as a kid. His Dad taught there. August 1947."

## ABOUT THE AUTHOR

From the First Edition by **Stanley L. Benjamin**, 1971

AS THE TITLE, *Through the Years*, SUGGESTS, THESE POEMS ARE THE accumulation of a lifetime—a lifetime, not outstanding in any way; but wonderfully interesting. It all began seventy-five years ago on a sandy, worn-out farm in southern Michigan, which had been taken up by the author's great-grandfather in 1835. The family was made up of hard-working pioneers who could never quite achieve financial success. They were never hungry, but the wolf was never far from the door.

The author attended a one-room school where his grandfather and father had been pupils before him. It must have required sacrifice by his father—his mother had died when he was twelve years old—to send him to high school in Constantine. But he did graduate from high school in 1913.

No one in the author's family had ever attended college. Both his mother and his father had taught in one-room rural schools, but this was at a time when a high school graduate could be certified to teach in such schools. Following high school, he sort of drifted from one job to another—Post Office Clerk, farm work, store clerk, lumber-jack, sawmill worker. (He was always thankful that he had a small part in the drama of the dying days of the lumber industry in Michigan.)

Then came the First World War. Without waiting for the draft, the author volunteered for service in the army. He did not get overseas, and most of his military service was on the Mexican border. After almost a year in service, he was still a "buck private." Then for no reason other than that he had a high-school diploma, he was selected to attend officers' training school. Much to his surprise, he finished in the top two percent of the young second lieutenants.

His gold bars did not have much influence on the course of the war. But they did have two important results in his own life.

1. He returned to Harbor Springs and married his young sweetheart.
2. He decided that when the war ended he would try to go to college. And the war was soon over.

FOLLOWING WORLD WAR ONE, THERE WAS NO G.I. HELP FOR VETERANS who might be ambitious for a college education. Moreover, a married college student was almost unheard of. But this young man was goaded by two spurs: He wanted to enter the ministry, and he wanted a college education. So with a wife and a very thin bank account, he enrolled in Albion College. (Before the four-year college course was finished, they had a family of two sons.)

During the years of drifting from one job to another, the author had worked for a while at shoe-repairing. In Albion he found a job working at this trade. It was not a very highly regarded occupation, but it was a job. And, he worked at it for four years. During his Junior and Senior years, he also served as student-pastor of a little Methodist church at Spring Arbor. In spite of the demands of a growing family plus two jobs, he managed to graduate in the "Class of 1924." In fact, his degree read, "With highest honors."

However, an event in his Senior year made it necessary that his life plans be changed. His father got into financial difficulties of such a nature that the son had to borrow a considerable sum of money to help him out of his trouble. The necessity to repay this debt seemed to bar the way for entry into the ministry. So his plans were changed and he entered Education instead.

His first teaching position was in the small town of Carsonville, in the Thumb of Michigan. His title was "superintendent"; but he taught five classes a day; coached foot-ball, basket-ball, base-ball and debate, and had charge of the Junior and Senior plays. Incidentally, he also added two more children—girls—to his growing family. After four years of this easy job the family moved on to South Rockwood, in the outer suburban area of Detroit. Those were the years of the great depression, and he was fortunate to have a job, even though he was not happy in that location.

After six years here, he was very glad to return to the Thumb as Superintendent at Croswell. These thirteen years might have been happy ones except for the fact that they included the years of the Second World War. His two oldest sons were in the service, and dozens of "his boys" from the school were overseas. It was said that the casualty rate among Croswell boys was one of the highest in the state.

The time came when it seemed best to make another move, this time to Galesburg in the southwestern part of Michigan. The most noteworthy achievement here was the uniting of two districts to form the Galesburg-Augusta Community Schools. This union was a pioneer of scores of similar consolidations which have since occurred.

Years were passing, and the author was beginning to think about retirement. He and his wife had decided that they wanted their retirement to be somewhere in Northern Michigan, with the area around Indian River as their first choice. So when he was offered the position of superintendent of the Inland Lakes School at Indian River, he resigned at Galesburg-Augusta and moved to the North Country. Three years here rounded out his career in education.

But another career was opening. The Congregational Church at Cheboygan was looking for a new minister. They asked the author to fill their pulpit one Sunday, not as a candidate but simply as a supply preacher. After the service, one of the deacons asked, "We do not know just when we will have a candidate coming in. Would you help us out a few Sundays until we do?" He agreed. After some three months of this arrangement, the author-preacher suggested that they should increase their effort to find a regular minister. The response of the church was to invite the author to become their regularly called minister. He was not an ordained minister, but following a term at Eden Seminary, the Michigan Conference agreed to ordain him. (He was perhaps the oldest man ever ordained by the Congregational Church in Michigan.) He served the Cheboygan Church for nearly nine years—the second-longest tenure of any minister in the nearly hundred years of the church's history. So in his older years (a polite way of saying "old age"), he found the career he had planned for his youth.

But the time came when it was apparent that the church needed the services of a younger man. Such a man was found, and the author and his wife have retired to their "Little Pink House in the Pines" at Indian River.

The poems which are included in *Through the Years* are the products of all of these years.

John Serell (b. 11 March 1894), Stilwell Frederick (b. 1 February 1899), and Stanley Langton (b. 19 September 1895), with their mother, Cora Belle (Langton) Benjamin (b. 31 August 1867). Cora Belle died of a brain aneurysm on 14 August 1907, at the age of 39.

William Henry Benjamin (b. 9 October 1866, d. 22 April 1936), Serell, Stanley and Stilwell, photographed while still living in St. Joseph Township, near Constantine, Michigan, not long after the death of their mother, Cora Belle.

Stanley, holding the flag, remained in Constantine to finish high school after the rest of the family moved to the recently abandoned Cobb and Mitchell lumber camp at Springvale, in Emmet County, Michigan, with plans to farm the land. After graduating from high school in 1913, Stanley worked many jobs—Post Office Clerk, farm work, store clerk, lumberjack, and sawmill worker.

Stanley wanted to go into the ministry but a series of personal setbacks for his father led him to a career in education instead.

Stanley's older brother John Serell Benjamin and his son, Ronald William Benjamin. Serell died of Influenza on 7 December 1918 while in military service in Oregon. His widow, La Verna Edna (Hammond) Benjamin, remarried John Campbell, a lighthouse keeper who worked at Grassy Island Lighthouse near Detroit, Huron Island Lighthouse on Lake Superior, and finally at Old Mackinac Point Lighthouse in Mackinaw City.

Lieutenant Stanley Benjamin in Little Rock, Arkansas, ca. 1918 (left), and (right) Stanley graduating from Albion College in 1924 with an A.B. in Education. Lillian made a trip to visit Stanley in Little Rock in November 1918, while he was still in the military. They had married 28 August 1918.

(Front row, center) Stanley's first job out of college was as a school superintendent in Carsonville, Michigan, where the family lived from 1924-1928. The position called upon jack-of-all-trades skills including teaching, coaching and directing theatre productions. This photo is an early class of graduates under his supervision.

Stanley Benjamin with his younger brother, Stilwell (Ben) Benjamin, ca. late 1940s, likely taken at a family wedding.

[TOP] Stanley and Lillian Benjamin, Rena Wilson Benjamin, and Ruth and Stilwell (Ben) Benjamin, gathered together in Croswell, Michigan, in 1938 around the time of opening of the Blue Water Bridge. Stan and Stilwell's father and Rena's husband, William, died in April of 1936. Rena was born on a farm in Howe, Indiana on 8 September 1894, and died 18 August 1950, when she was 55 years old.

[ABOVE] After moving to northern Michigan in 1913, Stanley's father William met and married Rena Wilson and they had four daughters. Stanley and his brother Stilwell (Ben) met up with their half-sisters Hilda, Maude, Ruth and Mary, in Croswell, Michigan, in 1938.

The six children of William Henry Benjamin, Hilda, Stanley, Mary, Ruth, Stilwell (Ben), and Maude. The photo is captioned, "Years Later." One son, Serell, had died in 1918.

[TOP] Stanley was school superintendent at Galesburg, Michigan, from 1947-1959.

[BOTTOM] Stanley and Lillian, far right, celebrated their 60th wedding anniversary on 28 August 1978. In this photo they are, from left to right, Ruth Edith Benjamin (Krieg), Maude Murray Benjamin (Gilmore), Mary Asenath Benjamin (Ford), and Hilda Marie Benjamin (Pridgeon). Also pictured is Ronald William Benjamin, son of Serell, Stanley's brother who died in 1918.

Stanley in a summery and congenial mood, 1968.

[TOP] From left to right, Ray (b. 1885), Hattie (Griffin) (b. 1863, d. 1913), Abbie (b. 1882), Edward T. Couch (b. 1853, d. 1917) and Elizabeth Velma Couch (b. 1887). Edward arrived in northern Michigan from Canada in 1872 to help build the railroads and homesteaded on Walloon Lake ca. 1874. Edward married Hattie in 1880 and a few years later they moved to Boyne City. Hattie was born in New York before moving to Boyne City as a girl with her family.

[BOTTOM] From left to right, Edward T. Couch, Alfred Vincent (b. 1901, d. 1991), Hattie and Lillian Mildred (b. 1897, d. 1989). Not long after this photo, Hattie was institutionalized at the Northern Michigan Asylum in Traverse City, where she remained the rest of her life. Alfred went to live with Henry and Elizabeth (Couch) Bacon, relatives who lived nearby. Lillian was moved from family to family before settling with her devout Christian sister, Velma. At some point Edward became a Latter Day Saint connected to the Mormons of Beaver Island, a transition that did not resonate well with his family.

Lillian Couch in a studio portrait taken in the E.E. Bowman Studio, Petoskey, Michigan, ca. 1905.

Lillian posed for this photo holding a certificate or diploma. She wears the gold bracelet giving to her by her father when she turned 16.

Lillian Couch with her coworkers at Wequetonsing, an exclusive Presbyterian summer resort in Harbor Springs. She is third from the left in the second row, wearing a white skirt and white shirtwaist, ca. 1915.

Lillian, third from the left, enjoying the shores of Lake Michigan on the beach near Harbor Springs. The photo was labeled only "Sun Fish" on the back. Lillian's sweet expression directly into the camera hints that it may have been Stanley taking the photograph, ca. 1917.

Lillian Couch enjoying a summer day in Harbor Springs with her friend Helen Keiser, ca. 1917.

Stanley Langton Benjamin married Lillian Mildred Couch on 28 August 1918 in Harbor Springs, Michigan. Stanley was still in the military and wearing his uniform.

Lillian and her friends show their patriotism ca. 1917 wwhile visiting the Benjamin family farm near Springvale, Michigan, while Stanley was away in military service for World War I. The back of the photo was labeled "Rookies" with Lillian Couch, Helen Keiser, and Miss Smith.

Stanley was athletic and enjoyed directing and performing in plays—and was also partial to a little drama in everyday life.

Stanley wrote on the back of this photo of Lillian Couch: "May 1917. She wasn't married then."

Stanley and Lillian shortly after they married in 1918, with nephew Vincent Fetters, nicknamed Curly, son of Bert and Elizabeth Velma (Couch) Fetters, of Harbor Springs. At this time, young boys were dressed differently and often had long hair, so people today often mistake boys for girls in period photographs.

Lillian and Stanley Benjamin at the wedding of Barbara and Ed Benjamin, in Ann Arbor, Michigan, 14 November 1953.

## INTRODUCTION

By **Stanley L. Benjamin**

I don't write poetry; I just write verse,
Some of it bad and some of it worse.
Sometimes it seems that words of mine
Stand up straight in perfect line
Just like well trained soldiers do.
That last line now is really true;
But just like soldiers made of lead,
These words of mine seem awfully dead.

You know to make a poem real
The poet's words have got to feel
Like a bunch of kids just out of school.
Forgetting every sort of rule
The words must leap and race and run,
Singing and laughing in their fun.
But my words don't. When the theme is gay
The poor things are too old for play.

This sounds terrible, but I think
A poet's words should take to drink—
Not drink such an awful lot
Like some silly, staggering sot—
But drink enough to forget all care,
And see a few things that are not there.
Now the words with which my verse is full
Are respectable—but deadly dull.

Now when a poet wants to write
About the beauty of the night,
His stealthy words should try to keep
The rustling breezes half asleep,
As they tip-toe in with quiet tread—
But my words shout to raise the dead.

My words know how they should perform,
Rumble and roar with the raging storm,
Flash like the stroke of lightning bright—
A razor cutting the beard of night.
They know! Yet somehow when I try
To write about a mountain high,
These stubborn words of mine just will
Persist in describing a little hill.

But if some critic should ever dare
These simple verses to compare
With what some regular poet wrote,
I'd grab the fellow by the throat
And choke until his face got red
And he took back what he had said;
For after all is said and done,
I write these verses just for fun.

Stanley L. Benjamin signing copies of Through the Years in the dining room of the Holmes' house in Lake City, Michigan, 1971.

PART 1
# JUST FOR THE KIDS

Puppy Pixie Penny, Dorothy, Lillian and Stanley explore the shore of Lake Louise with the first-time grandpa holding baby Lucinda (Cindy) Holmes. The photo also notes, "First picture of our Lake Louise Lot. July 14, 1948."

## *STRING BEAN*

*(Gramp started out to write a welcoming poem for each new grandchild; but when their number got to fourteen, he gave up. Here are a few of the verses.)*

My dear Lucinda Jean
Today we will talk about a common garden vegetable
   called the string bean.
Sometimes the bean
    Wears a coat of green,
       Sometimes a coat of yellow.
But whatever color coat he wears, you will find Mr. String Bean
   to be a very fine fellow.

Sometimes people say a girl is thin a string bean as;
But that is not the kind of a figure I am sure Lucinda Jean has.

String beans can be cooked about any way the cook may please;
But I like them best prepared with a thick cream sauce
   made with plenty of good strong cheese.
However little children have to eat string beans as a
   gooey, green mess put in little tin cans by Gerbers or Clapp,
So I don't blame kids when they spill the beans all of
   their mother's lap.

In planting his garden, string beans are Gramp's favorite seeds;
The bugs don't eat them, and they grow faster than the weeds.

## GRANDDAUGHTER NUMBER 2

Listen madam; Harken, mister!
Lucinda has a baby sister.
Harken, father; Harken mother!
No, she doesn't have a brother.
Another little cute deicer,
Boys are nice; but girls are nicer.

Some say an angel from the skies
Brought her here from paradise;
Some folks give the stork the credit,
And others say the doctor did it.
Whichever theory may be true,
There was one girl, but now there's two.

Two girls are twice as nice as one;
Double the trouble, double the fun.
Twice as many dolls to dress,
Twice as many clothes to press,
Twice as many mouths to feed,
Twice as many books to read.

Twice as many good-night kisses
For a pair of little misses.
Another little darling daughter
To cry at night for a glass of water.
Two little girls to defy the weather,
And have chicken-pox together.

Two times one are two red noses;
Two times ten are twenty toeses.
Tootsies little; tootsies big—
To market went this little pig.
Twice as many curls to comb—
This little piggy stayed at home.

Another grandchild has been born—
This little pig has an ear of corn.
Two girls are better far than one—
This poor little pig had none.
Two girls to sit on grandpa's knee—
This little pig said, "We, Wee, Weee!"

Listen madam; Harken, mister!
Lucinda has a baby sister.
Harken, father; Harken, mother!
Now she wants a baby brother.

THROUGH THE YEARS

## *TO THE FIRST GRANDSON*

*(Grandfathers are the most sedate people!)*

Yippi-ki-yi, and a couple of cheers!
Pass out the cigars and set up the beers.
Draw a red circle around the date.
Let's go out and celebrate.
Run down to the village and inform the people;
Ring the biggest bell in the tallest steeple.
Tell all the youngsters is shout for joy,
Our little grandchild is a boy.

Oh, little girls can be awfully nice,
And we like grand-daughters—once or twice.
Even three females are not bad, but
We feared that the stork was in a rut.
Sure, we love the little ladies tender;
But we wanted one of the rugged gender.
And yippi-ki-yi, that's what we got,
So thanks, old storkie, thanks a lot.

Rush to the biggest department store,
Buy out the place and then look for more.
No silly rattles or baby toys;
Buy him the stuff that's meant for boys.
Buy him a knife and an aeroplane,
A ball, a bat, and an electric train.
Buy him a holster and a big six-shooter.
Maybe he needs a motor-scooter.

Get him a rifle—a twenty-two,
An Indian suit and a red canoe.
Buy him a wicker fishing creel,
A casting rod and a spinning reel.
I'll bet already the black-haired scamp
Wants to go fishing with his gramp
I can tell by the way he wiggles and squirms
He'll be an expert in digging worms.

So yippi-ki-yi for the latest grandchild!
Let's give three cheers for the eight-pound-man-child,
Whose grand-dad boasts from dawn to dark
Of this wonder of wonders, grandson Mark.

Stanley and Lillian spent several Christmases at the Holmes' house in Lake City, Michigan. Here grandson number one, Mark William Holmes, is eager to get a Christmas present from his father, Herbert.

Stanley George Benjamin at an early meeting of Stanley Langton Benjamin, ca. 1953.

## *TO STAN*

Hi, young fellow, with your grandpappy's name
Let's you and your grandpa play a little game.
It really is an old, old game men call the relay race,
One runner runs a little while, then another takes his place.

The first contestant carries an emblematic scroll
And hands it to the second man to carry to the goal.
Now, Stan, you and your granddad will play this relay game;
You'll be the second runner to carry on a name.

For a while, as you get started, he will run here at your side,
So that he can try to help you to catch a winning stride.
And maybe he can show you the pitfalls in the track,
And how best to avoid them when there is no turning back.

He may help you see the wonder of the course that you will run,
The splendor of the autumn hills, the glow of setting sun,
The beauty in the spring-time of blossom-burdened trees;
To learn to hear God's whisper in the murmur of the breeze.

And when the rules for running
To you have all been shown,
He will sit down by the race track,
And you will run alone.

You will run a swifter race than he has ever run;
You will do important works such as he has never done.
You will live more nobly than he could ever live;
You will give more to others than he ever had to give.

You will win tougher battles than he had the strength to fight;
You will write enduring poems such as he could never write.
You will preach inspiring sermons that he could never preach;
Teach more true and profound lessons that he could ever teach.

And Yonder in the Grandstand,
Beyond the fartherest blue
An old man will be watching
And be mighty proud of you.

## *CLAUDIA CADE*

Another visit the stork has paid
And brought a bundle named Claudia Cade.
Claudia Cade, Oh, Claudia Cade,
After the hospital bill is paid,
And after the doctor has got his due,
Your Daddy is going to look at you
And say, "I'm broke, but what do I care.
I'm richer than a millionaire."

Also your granddad welcomes you
To his lusty, growing, grandchild crew;
While all your cousins, uncles and aunts
Are eagerly waiting for their chance
To join in the joyous, glad parade
And bid you welcome, Claudia Cade.

## *JENNIFER RUTH*

Jennifer Ruth, Oh, Jennifer Ruth!
Tell us the truth, dear Jennie.
How much would you have if you held in each hand
Three nickels, two dimes, and a penny?

Jennifer Ruth, Oh, Jennifer Ruth!
Tell us the truth, dear Jennie.
Why do chickens have feathers galore,
While children don't have any?

Jennifer Ruth, oh, Jennifer Ruth!
Tell us the truth, dear Jennie.
How do fire-flies light their lamps,
And why are there so many?

And Jennifer Ruth, dear Jennifer Ruth,
If you don't know all the answers,
Tell the brownies to tell the elves
To ask the fairy dancers.

## RICHARD JOHN*

Oh, Richard John, you're a lucky lad
    With a pretty Ma and a handsome Dad,
And four grandparents who try to win
    The accolade of your toothless grin.

But listen, young fellow, we want you to know
    Of another Richard, who long ago
Left a home that to him was dear
    For the rugged life of a pioneer.

We want you to hear the heroic tale,
    How he traveled the rough, wild forest trail,
Hour after hour; day after day,
    Toward a land of promise far away.

Till he found the spot that he had in mind,
    Where the soil was rich and the weather kind
He unyoked his oxen, unleashed his dogs,
    And built his cabin of hand-hewn logs.

Swinging his axe in the dewey morn,
    He cleared his acres and planted his corn.
Broad grew his fields and green his sod,
    As he plowed his furrows and worshipped God.

He left for us a better land,
    With fertile fields and cities grand,
With churches and schools and the right to be
    Happy and healthy, contented and free.

So as you race through your boyhood years
    With their pleasures and triumphs, and their tears,
Think of this grand-sire of long ago,
    And remember how much to him we owe.

---

\* *Named after his great-great-great-great grandfather, Richard Benjamin, born in New York State in 1770. Migrated to Michigan in 1835.*

Kim Knudtzon was four months old when she met her grandparents, Stanley and Lillian, in 1955.

## "K"

Kome all you kousins, come and see
    The youngest and sweetest, Kendra Marie.
With one of her dainty dresses on
    She won't be nude though she is Knudtzon.

K stands for Kurt; K stands for Kim.
    Kim is a her, and Kurt a him.
So of the K's there now are three;
    And the newest K is Kendra Marie.

Yes, Kendra Marie is a dainty miss;
    Give her a hug and give her a kiss.
Although there soon will be one more,
    Hurray for number ten and four.

## NUMBER 15

We couldn't rest 'til we had seen
    George Wesley, grandchild No. Fifteen.
So, though the icy road was long;
    So, though the March wind blew full strong;
So, though the blizzing blizzard blist,
    We drove to Indianapolist.

Now that we've seen him, we confess
    He looks a lot like all the rest.
Now this may make some angry mothers,
    To say that one looks like the others;
But this I'm sure is really true,
    For all the rest are handsome too.

Of course, his parents will insist
    That Wes is a good Methodist;
But I confess I wonder why:
    A Methodist is always dry,
While this young fellow, I would bet,
    A dozen times a day votes wet.

But just the same, we're mighty proud
    Of all our thirty-legged crowd.

## *TWO YARDS*

Our neighbor's yard is broad and green,
    With formal beds of flowers rare;
And well-trimmed shrubs grown in between—
    He gives them hours and hours of care.

To have such flowers I've often tried—
    The baby picks them as they bloom,
And with a look of joy and pride,
    Brings a bouquet for Mother's room.

Their lawn is like a velvet rug,
    Surrounded by an iron fence.
In it no holes are ever dug.
    It makes ours look like thirty cents.

The grass in our front yard is worn,
    And unwashed dishes from mud-pies
Sometimes the shady spots adorn,
    And scattered toys offend the eyes.

They say the kids have spoiled our lawn;
    And yet when I awake from rest,
And both yards sparkle in the dawn,
    I know that I like our yard best.

THROUGH THE YEARS

## *ROCKET TRIP*

All Aboard!
          Away we go
For a trip among the stars.
We're going to visit Venus
And take a look at Mars.

Oh, Venus is a lady
In a low-neck gown;
But Mars, a red-eyed fighter
Who wears an ugly frown.

And when we stop at Saturn,
We will race around its rings;
Then play tag with little Mercury,
A messenger with wings.

If we overtake a comet,
We will grab it by the tail.
(For pulling tails on comets
Can one be put in jail?)

And if we should get hungry
Or thirsty in our play,
We will find the Little Dipper
And drink the Milky Way.

Oh we will have a lot of fun
A-sailing through the sky;
And all the little baby stars
Will smile as we whiz by.

Of course we'll stop to say "Hello"
To our jolly friend, the moon.
Tonight he's just a sliver;
But he'll be much fatter soon.

## CARROTS

I know some girls with yellow curls
    Whom folks call "Carrot-top";
And every time they call them that,
    I try to make them stop.

Because they really ought to know,
    If they have ever seen
A row of carrots growing,
    That a carrot-top is green.

A carrot-top is green, all right,
    As anyone should know.
They make a mighty pretty sight
    All growing in a row.

But the yellow part of carrots
    Grows underneath the ground.
I hope you like to eat them
    'Cause scientists have found

Something in the yellow carrot
    Helps improve a person's sight,
Makes her eyes a whole lot stronger
    For seeing things at night.

So if you want to go out nights,
    As most young ladies do,
You had better eat your carrots
    When your mother tells you to.

## *PRETTY LITTLE PUSSY CAT*

Pretty little pussy cat.
    Black and White.
Roaming fields and meadows
    In the pale moon-light.

Mother tried to catch him;
    How Mama stunk !
Pretty little pussy cat
    Was
        a
            skunk.

## *PASSING YEARS*

Tell us a story, Daddy,
Just one little story, please
No, Kiddies. Your daddy's too tired.
No story tonight—and don't tease.

How many years ago was it?
Long ago I lost track of their flight.
I am tired. But how gladly I'd hear
That *tell us a story* tonight.

THROUGH THE YEARS

## *THE POTATO*

Consider, Bud, the lowly spud,
    Called also the potater.
To prove his worth to this old earth
    Don't take a great debater.

He has about a dozen eyes.
    To us this seems sufficient.
So this may be a big surprise—
    His sight is quite deficient.

Though he is weak at seeing,
    He is strong at being seen.
He's served in many a dainty dish.
    That's set before the queen.

He is eaten in the summer;
    He is eaten in the spring.
He's eaten by the president;
    He's eaten by the king.

He is eaten in the palace;
    He is eaten in the jail;
He is eaten by prime ministers,
    And prisoners out on bail.

They eat him in the army and
    They eat him in the navy;
We eat him every Sunday, mashed
    With roast beef gravy.

Some people whoop for potato soup,
    While others prefer to bake;
And have you tried hot French fried
    With sizzling sirloin steak?

Yes, the spud is an aristocrat,
    Not just a common tater.
If Doc says that he makes you fat,
    Doc's a prevaricator.

So give a cheer for the spud so dear.
    Learn all you can about him.
Remember, Lad, it would be bad
    To try to do without him.

# PART 2
# LET'S GO FISHING

## *TROUT FEVER*

When I smell the flowers of spring
    And hear the first brave robin sing,
It is like a voice that calls me
    From a land that's far away,
From a land whose clear, cold streams
    Fill my thoughts and haunt my dreams;
And it's there I want to be
    The First of May.

There's one little stream that babbles
    In and out among the shadows,
Gurgling with a laughter
    Like children in their play.
And the trees that grow above it
    Bend down as if they love it;
And it's there I want to be
    The First of May.

Round a bend the waters sweep
    To a pool that's still and deep,
Where the cedars, crowding round it,
    Keep the noon-day sun away.
There the king of all trout hides,
    Through the shadowy depths he glides,
And I'm going back to get him
    When it comes the First of May.

So I'll leave the rush and hurry;
    I'll forget my care and worry.
I'm going to lock the office
    And throw the key away,
For that little stream is calling;
    What care I if rain is falling,
I am hitting for the Cedar
    On the season's opening day.

Stanley and Lillian both enjoyed fishing the streams and inland lakes of northern Michigan.

## *BIOLOGY*

Little fishy, in the brook,
    We read about you in our book,
All about your family life,
    How your little fishy wife
Lay her eggs beside a stone,
    And then you do your part alone.
For such arrangement some might wish;
    But I am glad I'm not a fish.

Many of the Benjamin grandchildren recalled Stanley rising early to fish before breakfast, heading off to his secret fishing places.

## LONE FISHERMAN

When I am fishing on some woodland stream,
Though I may fish apart, I never seem
To be alone, for my old smelly creel,
This battered old felt hat, my rod and reel,
Are like old friends of whom I've fonder grown.
With all of these, how could one feel alone.

And as I walk beside the shady creek,
Her eddies smile like dimples on the cheek
Of laughing maiden, and her gurgling song
Sings a low lullaby for a throng
Of woodland creatures who her thickets share,
The ruffed grouse, the deer, the snow-shoe hare.

One day last summer on the Manistee,
After a noonday nap, I woke to see
A mother deer beside her spotted fawn
Come down to drink. Another time at dawn
A hummingbird poised in her flashing grace
Above a flower not two feet from my face.

'Twas on the North Branch of the Boyne, I think,
I one day had a full-grown hungry mink
Come to my very feet along a limb
To carry off the trout I threw at him.
And oft at evening, from some nearby hill,
I hear the plaintive call of whip-poor-will.

And yet sometimes I have heard people say,
"How can he bear to fish alone all day?"

Stanley fishing in White Lake, Ontario, Canada, 1967. The photo by Al Bradfield is also inscribed, "Stan is Happy. Fishin' was good!" From boyhood through old age, he never lost his love of fishing.

## ANGLER'S TRAGEDY

He used to like to fish on those rare days
    When he could leave his work an hour or two;
Or, rising in the early morning's haze,
    Tramp by some stream drenched with the sparkling dew.

His tackle, just a sinker, line and hook—
    No gaudy lures or gaily colored fly—
To him these were but things at which to look
    His slender purse could never hope to buy.

And yet the joy those hours alone could bring!
    Hours snatched from labor for the healing balm
Of woodland streams, to hear a wild bird sing,
    Or feel the peace that comes with sun-set's calm.

He made his pile, as some such fellows do;
    Has all the wealth a person could desire.
They say he's worth a million, maybe two;
    Still in his prime but able to retire.

The day arrived of which he used to dream.
    Day after day, as once had been his wish,
He motored with his chauffeur to some stream,
    And hour on hour did nothing else but fish.

His tackles now the finest wealth could buy;
    His rod was made of choicest split bamboo,
His line of silk. Imported was his fly.
    He bought each lure the dealer said was new.

And yet somehow he could not catch the joy
    That had been his fishing days of yore.
His tackle gathered dust. He told his boy,
    "I don't care much for fishing any more."

## *BIG TROUT FROM A TINY STREAM*

I have fished the famed Au Sable
    And many a lesser stream
Whose names like sweetest music
    Fill the sleeping angler's dream.

And in fishing, I have found in them
    The triumphs anglers seek;
But they never give a greater thrill
    Than one small, nameless creek.

It was just a spring-fed trickle,
    And it didn't really seem
That any fish worth catching
    Could live in such a stream.

But I found among the alders
    One place, where still and deep
The water gurgling round a bend,
    Paused for a while to sleep.

There hidden by the meadow grass
    That grew along the bank,
I dropped my bait into the pool,
    And as it slowly sank,

The sleeping stream was awakened,
    And that little, sheltered nook
Was lashed to sudden fury
    As the great trout felt the hook.

But his battle ground was narrow,
    And he could not rush nor leap,
Nor shake from out his quivering jaw
    The barb that bit so deep.

The fight was quickly over,
    As I proudly lifted out
From that little meadow brooklet
    A two-pound speckled trout.

I've caught other fish far bigger;
    But none gave a greater thrill
Than catching such a trout as that
    From such a tiny rill.

I suppose that on life's journey,
    As we run our daily race,
We may find the greatest triumphs
    In some unsuspected place.

## *THE ONE THAT GOT AWAY*

'Though you've caught your speckled beauties
    Along about the first of May,
Yet the trout you most remember
    Is the one that got away.

Still you hear the river's murmur,
    See again the evening gray,
When you felt those fierce, wild rushes
    Of the one that got away.

And that memory keeps tugging,
    So you're going back next May
Just to have another battle
    With the one that got away.

Fish we catch are weighted and measured
    And that weight they have to stay.
No one knows the weight nor measure
    Of the one that got away.

So the one we almost landed
    Keeps on growing day by day.
None can prove that we are lying
    About the one that got away.

So in life, though many triumphs
    Deck our brows with garlands gay,
Still we have a secret longing
    For the one that got away.

PART 3
# NATURE

## FAREWELL TO THE FOREST

One day last spring I saw two lumber-jacks
Cut the last tree in what, ten years before,
Had been a forest, stretching mile on mile.
A mighty pine it was, full five feet through,
And towering straight and high like some tall mast.
Two-hundred years it had defied the blast
Of winter; but now to its base there came
Long John, the Pole, and Big Swede Anderson.
Their axes swing; and then the singing saw
Eats to its heart. A quiver shakes the trunk.
Slowly at first begins the solemn fall,
Then moving faster through a mighty arc,
It crashes to the earth. The echoes die.
An epoch has been finished in the wild.

And as that towering pin crashed to the earth,
I closed my eyes, and saw as in a dream
The mighty drama of the woods unfold.

I saw the forest stretching mile on mile,
Untouched by human hands; its silent aisles
Untrod by human foot, save when alone
The red-skinned hunter stalked his wary prey.
Then came the first white man, the forest cruiser,
Seeking the cream of all this boundless wealth,
Seekthing the tracts wherein the pines grew tallest,
Where rushing rivers would provide a path
To float the fallen timbers to the mill.

The first tree fell, first victim of the strife,
Relentless man against the boundless woods.
I saw the camps, bunk-houses long and low,
The mess shack, stables--all aglow with life.
A hundred men full bearded, hard as iron,
In mackinaws that matched the rainbow's hues,
Set out before the dawn, each to his task,
Some laughing, others always with a curse,
The choppers, sawyers, swampers and the rest--
No place for weaklings here, but strong man all.
Long ere the sun had topped the esatern hills,
The steady ring of axe, the whine of saw,
Are heard like music on the cold, clear air.

I saw great loaded sleighs swing down the road
To where out on the river's ice were piled
Mountains of logo to wait the first spring thaw.
The spring rains come; the river starts to rise;
The ice bridge weakens. Then one soft warm day
The forest trembles like an earthquake shock;
A roar like thunder smites the listening ear.
The log jam breaks, the drive is on its way.
Out on the swirling stream the river men,
Nimble as cats, leap far from log to log,
Plodding some laggard toward the swifter flow,
Pulling the key log from a threatening jam,
Each moment daring death to do its worst.
Swiftly the drive moves downward toward the lake,
Where like some monster waits the empty mill.

I saw again the steaming pond, the steady stream of logs
Drawn up to feed the ever hungry saws;
The piles of fresh white lumber by the lake,
Waiting the bellowing freighters which would soon
Transport it far to build a nation's homes.
Once more I smell the odor of the pine,
The fragrance of the maple, birch and fir,
Scents which the lumberman, however old,
Once having known, will always know and love.

These were the acts I saw in a dream;
The actors, iron men who knew no fear.
But now the show is ended; nevermore
The ringing axe shall wake the forest glade.
The once green hills, denuded burned and bare,
Lift boney hands to cold unyielding sky.
Where stood the camp, one now can scarcely find
A single trace, except the scattered heap
Of rusting cans among the tangled thorns.
The screaming whistle of the logging train
No more shall echo through the gathering dusk.
The rushing river carries now but foam;
The drive of pine will never come again.
Down by the lake a few charred, fallen beams,
Some rusted, twisted rods alone remain
To mark the spot where stood the busy mill.

So with the falling of that last great pine,
The curtain fell.
The drama of the woods has reached its end.
The forest is no more.

## "TIMBER"

Did you ever hear that warning cry
That sounds as a great tree starts to fall?
When the tall pine trembles against the sky,
The lumber-jacks stand back and call,
   "Timber-r-r! Tim-m-mber!"

When the air is clear and the day is still
And the cold snow sparkles all about,
The sound returns from the distant hill,
And echoes answer the hearty shout,
   "Timber-r-r! Tim-m-mber!"

Such was the day when the last pine fell.
One moment it towered green and fair,
Then bowed in the forest's last farewell,
As that cry rang out on the sparkling air,
   "Timber-r-r! Tim-m-mber!"

The echoes fainter and fainter grew,
As if the barren hillsides knew
That never again would the Northland hear
That shout of warning sounding clear,
   "Timber-r-r! Tim-m-mber!"

## DEER SEASON

'Twas mid October, and the slopes below
    Were rich with aspen's wealth of yellow gold.
And on the hills the crimson maples glowed,
    As if their flame would ward off winter's cold.

We walked together up the woodland trail,
    Which years before the lumbermen had made;
But now, once more, the trees met overhead,
    Giving the road a day-time twilight shade.

Then on the hill we saw the sun again,
    The open fields of Old Man Bailey's place,
Long since deserted, turning back to brush,
    Like stubby beard on an unshaven face.

Long years ago Old Bailey cleared the land,
    Planted an orchard; and his clan had tried
To wrest a living from the sandy soil.
    They gave it up when Old Man Bailey died.

Deserted homesteads do not long remain;
    The house had burned; the barns had tumbled down.
The younger Baileys did not seem to care.
    They were too busy with their work in town.

Nothing remained except the apple trees
    That once had been Old Bailey's special pride,
And even now, in spite of long neglect,
    Bore fruit as rosy as a blushing bride.

We planned to carry home enough for pies—
    Deserted orchards are a common wealth
Whose fruit belongs to him who picks it up.
    There is no need to gather is by stealth.

But Mary stopped as if afraid to move,
    For she had seen that we were not alone.
Beneath the Pippin tree there stood three deer,
    A doe, an antlered buck, a fawn half-grown.

They had not seen us, but they heard some sounds,
    And raised their heads to see from whence it came,
They stood like statues in the settling sun,
    Or living pictures with the woods their frame.

Yet more than statues, more than pictures they;
    They were the woods from which they had come forth;
They were the forest's sunshine and its shade;
    They were the living spirit of the North.

To us they were incarnate Life itself;
    They were the actors of a show sublime.
How long we stood there we will never know;
    Such ecstasy as ours knows naught of time.

Such ecstasy one can not long endure,
    And I was first to feel its crushing strain.
I clapped my hands. An instant they were gone,
    Their flight like music of Life's glad refrain.

They cleared the lilac bushes with a bound,
    Spurred more by joy of living than by fear.
We stood as if before the throne of God,
    And watched them cross the road and disappear.

        \*    \*    \*

'Tis mid November and the leaves are gone.
    The wooded hills, denuded now and gray,
Reecho to the sound of rifle shots.
    Deer hunting season opened yesterday.

THROUGH THE YEARS

This afternoon the southward trek began.
    Successful hunters homeward make their way.
And on the tops of Cadillacs and Jeeps
    Are spread their trophies in a proud display.

Three gutted carcasses, like sacks of sand,
    Ride on the fenders of one ancient car,
That races drunken along the road.
    Their heads loll loosely with each jolting jar.

Those agile limbs are stiffened now in death,
    That sprang away so swiftly in alarm—
A doe, a buck, a fawn. They might have been
    The three we saw on Old Man Bailey's farm.

            \*    \*    \*

The sky is overcast; the grieving clouds
    Shed their soft tears upon the earth below.
In the dim woods there sounds a funeral dirge
    As through the trees the mourning north winds blows.

And in the low-roofed tavern by the road,
    Nimrods whose hunt thus far has been in vain
Sit drinking beer before an open fire,
    And curse the moaning wind and weeping rain.

## *FOREST TRAIL*

The magic wand of memory brings to me
A misty morning in the dew-drenched wood,
A forest trail through cool depths of shade,
The fluted columns of the towering pine,
Patches of sunlight on the forest floor,
A lovely land that was—but is no more.

The vision fades, and in its place I see
A sandy road between the sun baked hills;
Fire-blackened stumps, each one a monument
That marks the death of some tall towering tree.
The shimmering heat, the choking dust clouds mock
The cool, moist trail I saw in memory.

## TO A TRAILING ARBUTUS

You dainty white and pinkish posies,
I'd think that you would freeze your toesies,
You bloom so early in the spring
Before the bluebirds start to sing,
Before the buds swell in the trees,
Ere he-men change to B.V.D.'s

Before the rushes start to rush,
Or winter's snow banks turn to slush,
Before we let the fire go out,
Ere shivering anglers try for trout;
Beneath your blanket of dead leaves deep
You waken from your winter's sleep.

You waken and yawn in the warm spring sun,
And as the sap begins to run,
Your waxy leaves explore their way
Into the light; and then one day
We notice in the swamp a sweet perfume,
And say, "It must be spring; arbutus is in bloom."

There are other odors that we like to smell;
Roses are fragrant; violets are swell;
Lilacs are languorous, and there are, we're told,
Synthetic perfumes worth their weight in gold.
But none of these is worthy to compare
With your faint sweetness on the soft spring air.

The cry of wild geese in their northward flight,
The piping frogs that soothe the sleepy night,
Poplars on a hilllside turning green,
A housewife cleaning rooms already clean
Or changing paper on the pantry shelf,
Are signs of spring: But you are Spring itself.

It is no wonder then we love you so;
The wonder is the way our love we show.
Spurred by that love, into the swamp we hie.
To tear up root and stem and let you die.
Your story is a sad one to relate,
The flowers we love we soon exterminate.

## HILL FOLKS AND PLAINS PEOPLE

Give me a home by the side of a hill
Where the rocks are hard and the winds blow chill,
    And the tall pines sigh in the wintry blast.
There let me live through the changing years
While the rain of spring falls like sorrow's tears
    Till the summer's warmth shall come at last.

There I would live when the autumn days
Soften each peak with October's haze,
    And the maples scarlet and yellow grow.
There in my hill-encircled home,
I would watch the snows of winter come,
    And hear the blasts that his trumpets blow.

Let me climb to some peak in the early morn,
And watch while a bright new day is born,
    Till the strength of the hills is born in me.
Gazing far over the wooded vale,
Breasting the sweep of the hill-top gale,
    Let me stand alone, exultant, free.

The slope may be steep and the soil unkind,
But here in the rugged hills I find
    As my plow share cuts through the stubborn sod,
A peace and beauty unmarred by men,
The strength and courage to stive again
    That come to a man alone with God.

        \*   \*   \*

Let me dwell on a wide and fertile plain,
Where the soil is deep and the fields of grain
    Stretch off as far as the eye can see,
For the hills are rocky, sandy and steep;
Their winters are long, and their snows are deep
    And life in the hills is not for me.

Here as I view these acres wide,
My heart will swell with honest pride;
    Pride in the furrows my hands have turned,
The golden harvest my toils have earned,
    For the fields and the harvest are my own.

And worker in factory, store or bank,
Whatever may be his wealth or rank,
    Will look to me for his daily bread;
And not to the hills, where weary toil
Can wrest but want from the meager soil,
    For from the plains the world is fed.

        \*    \*    \*

Yes. The grain to feed the city's throng
    Must come from the plains, I suppose;
But the child of the hills writes poetry
    While the child of the plains lives prose.

## *ALONE*

Lonely?
In my wild northland I have often spent
A winter week alone—and been content.
Miles from the nearest human dwelling place,
Day after day I saw no human face.
My work by day, a book before the fire
At night, were all the friends I could desire.

Lonely?
There in the silence of the winter night
I heard a coyote howl. The northern light
Wrote its weird messages across the sky.
The low-hung stars seemed to proclaim that I
Was not alone, as twinkling they looked down,
Like lighted windows of some friendly town.

Lonely?
The morning sun turned the frost covered trees
To jewelled palaces. Mid scenes like these
How could a man be lonely? Far away
I heard the friendly quarreling of the jay,
And rabbit tracks around my cabin door
Announced my visitors of the night before.

Lonely? Yes!
When, in search of gold, in quest of fame,
I left my poor wild northern home and came
To walk along the thronging city street,
Where I see on the face of each I meet
The look that calls me *stranger*. Here indeed
I am alone. I feel the bitter need
For friendship; and alas, there is no friend.

## *STORM OVER LAKE LOUISE*

The air is still; all nature holds her breath.
A silence audible broods o'er the lake.
The silver aspen leaves are still as death
An unfelt tremor seems the earth to shake.

The billowing storm the western heaven fills,
Gray, dark and menacing as death's cold shroud.
The rumbling thunder rolls from distant hills;
The flashing lightning leaps from cloud to cloud.

Out on the lake one big drop make a splash--
Another, and another, faster still.
A steady patter; then a sudden crash
And falling rain obscures the nearby hill.

## *EVENING ON LAKE LOUISE*

An hour ago the lake danced in the breeze.
The Breeze has died; the dancing waves now sleep
Beneath a mirror. Overhanging trees
Are each reflected in the waters deep.

A single cloud float high above the lake,
Pink with the good-night kiss of parting day.
A lone trout leaps; the ripples gently break
The glassy surface and then fade away.

## *OCTOBER*

A week ago the maple in the field,
Like royalty was clad in robes of gold.
But now with naked trunk and shaking limbs revealed
A chorus girl, she shivers in the cold.

## *TRAILING ARBUTUS*

You flash no dazzling colors gay
Above you wet, cold bed,
Where yesterday the snow banks lay,
And still the leaves lie dead.

You have no lofty stem of pride
To lift your bloom on high
Beneath your waxy leaves you hide,
And in seclusion lie.

In you the virtues of the meek
Add modesty to grace;
Yet every spring the children seek
Your humble hiding place.

## *BAY-VIEW SUNSET*

The sun in the west as he sank to his rest,
Tired from the labor of day,
Paused ere he slept, and while soft shadows crept,
Gave his warm good-night kiss to the bay.

Every evening before for an eon or more
She has met him as homeward he rushes;
Still her wave-dimpled cheek his kiss seems to seek,
And still like a virgin she blushes.

And as the glow fades until darkness pervades,
And she waits for his kiss of the morrow,
The silence that falls as a whip-poor-willl calls
Is happiness mingled with sorrow.

## *TEN SOUNDS I LOVE TO HEAR*

1. The rustle of walking through dry oak leaves.
2. The call of a loon on a wild, lonely lake.
3. The rumble of distant thunder.
4. The patter of rain on a tin roof.
5. The whisper of a soft wind in a towering pine.
6. Christmas carolers singing "Holy Night"
7. The drumming of a partridge in the deep woods.
8. The rain song of an early robin.
9. The lusty cry of a new-born baby.
10. The sunset song of a hermit thrush.

## *TWO MONTHS*

October was a spendthrift
   Who threw his gold away.
In every hollow of the grove,
   Knee deep the treasure lay.

But November is a miser,
   When chilling north winds blow,
She wraps her gold in silence
   And buries it with snow.

## WINTER NIGHTS

Some winter nights are wandering nights,
    While some are meant for home.
When stars are bright, the northern lights
    Call hardy souls to roam.
But when the rain pounds on the pane,
    And drifts pile high and higher,
The wind's wild shriek invites us seek
    A seat beside the fire.

So if the night is clear and bright,
    Frost twinkling on the snow,
If tree tops trace their shadowy lace
    Upon the white below,
Down slippery slide our skis will glide,
    Frost tingling every cheek;
On singing steel we'll swing and wheel
    Along the frozen creek.

But if storms growl and north winds howl,
    If blizzards rage and roar,
With laughter bright we'll fill the night
    An open fire before;
With game and song the whole night long
    We'll mock the blustery weather,
For winter nights are always bright
    As long as we're together.

Stanley and Lillian raised six creative and active children. Here she already had her hands full with the first four, from left to right, Robert, Norma, Dorothy and Edward, ca. 1927.

The Benjamin boys, from left to right, Edward Leroy, Robert Serell, and William Howard, ca. 1935.

The Benjamin girls, from left to right, Norma Lillian, Dorothy Jean, and Helen Ilda, ca. 1935.

Caring for six children was a full-time job for Lillian. Youngest daughter, Dorothy, recalled that when she was small her parents sent out their laundry to be done, but then Stan brought home a washing machine and the work fell to Lillian, photo ca. 1935.

Family outings, like this trip in 1937, involved time at the beach, picnics, and overnights in rustic accommodations. The Benjamin family lived within five miles of Lake Huron, but also had family they often visited who lived near Lake Michigan.

Robert Serell Benjamin, shortly after graduating from high school. Born 24 September 2021, died 14 May 2006.

Robert Serell Benjamin married Gladys Irene Phillips on 24 June 1950, at Foundry Methodist Church, in Washington, D.C.

Edward Leroy Benjamin, in service with the merchant marine in World War II. Born 21 February 1923, died 11 June 2007.

Edward Leroy Benjamin married Barbara Jane Pugsley, 14 November 1953, in Ann Arbor, Michigan.

Dorothy Jean Benjamin high school graduation photo from Croswell, Michigan. Born 27 March 1925, died 14 May 2014.

Dorothy Jean Benjamin married Herbert Everett Holmes on 28 December 1945, in Croswell, Michigan, two months after Herbert returned from military service in World War II. At the far left is Ruth (Smythe) Brown, a life-long friend Dorothy met her freshman year at Michigan State College. Once married, Dorothy took "Benjamin" as her middle name.

Norma Lillian Benjamin, high school graduation photo from Croswell, Michigan. Born 3 December 1926, died 6 November 2019.

Norma Lillian Benjamin and Richard Luke Cade wedding, 24 June 1949, East Lansing, Michigan. After getting married she changed her name to Norma Benjamin Cade.

Helen Ilda Benjamin high school graduation photo from Croswell, Michigan. Born 23 November 1928, died 11 November 2015.

Helen Ilda Benjamin married Kenneth Knudtzon on 17 September 1949, in Galesburg, Michigan.

William Howard Benjamin, high school graduation photo from Galesburg, Michigan. Born 10 June 1931, died 8 September 2013.

Stanley and Lillian with William Howard Benjamin and Esther Ann Gillig at Bill and Esther's wedding on 28 December 1966, at the Bavarian Inn in Frankenmuth, Michigan.

A family gathering in Harbor Springs, Michigan, in 1937. Front: Norma, Dorothy, Helen, Hilda and Bill; back: Lillian, Ed, Maude, Rena, Ronald William, Ruth, Stan and Bob.

The extended family of Stanley and his brothers, Serell and Stilwell, gathered for the opening of the Blue Water Bridge in Port Huron, in 1938. Left to right, Bob, Helen, Ronald William, Dorothy, Cora, Stilwell (Ben) Jr., Elizabeth, Norma, and, in front, Bill.

[TOP] Stanley and Lillian moved many times during their marriage, maintaining a sparse home. Gathered together in 1940 to read and listen to the radio, are Dorothy, Bill, Stanley, Helen, Lillian, and Norma, with the family dog, Pago, in her lap.

[BOTTOM] Bob and Dorothy teamed together (see "B and D" in upper right corner) to create a cartoon rendition of the Benjamin family for this World War II era, 1941 Christmas card, capturing the spirit of each family member.

Benjamin family Christmas, Galesburg, Michigan, 1947. Back row, Dorothy, Lillian, Stanley, seven-week old Lucinda Holmes, and Bob; front row, Norma, Helen, Bill and Ed.

The Benjamin children gathered at Norma and Dick's wedding in East Lansing, 24 June 1949. From left to right and in the order of their ages, Bill, Helen, Norma, Dorothy, Ed and Bob.

Stanley and Lillian's 60th wedding anniversary, August 1978. From left to right, Bob, Ed, Helen, Norma, Lillian, Dorothy, Stanley and Bill.

All of the Benjamin kids with their spouses in the kitchen of Herbert and Dorothy Holmes, on E. Cass Street in Cadillac, Michigan. ca. 1979-1982. Back row, left to right, Barb and Ed Benjamin, Esther and Bill Benjamin, Bob and Nancy Benjamin, Herbert Holmes, Helen and Ken Knudtzon, Dick Cade. In front, Lillian Benjamin, Dorothy Holmes, and Norma Cade.

PART 4
# A BIT OF NONSENSE NOW AND THEN

## *THE EVOLUTION OF A GOLFER*

**1932**

Of all the silly, senseless things on earth, it seems to me
The silliest is this game called golf. How anyone can see
Any sense, or rhyme, or reason in such a foolish waste
Of his time and of his money; or have such childish taste
As to spend long hours perspiring in summer's boiling heat
Just to chase a little ball around, has really got me beat.

We've got a neighbor down the street who must be half insane.
Try to find him any afternoon and you will try in vain,
Unless you drive through dust and heat out to the Country Club,
Where it's ten to one you'll find him playing with some other dub.
And if he isn't playing, you can pretty surely know
He'll be out behind the clubhouse taking lessons from the pro.

And after you have found him, it don't do you any good.
Instead of talking business like any sane man would,
He starts at once to tell you about the lucky drive
He had on number seven; how he missed his putt on five
When he might have had a birdie. And hours more of the same.
I saw that anyone's an idiot who plays that crazy game.

**1934**

Well! I went out and tried it. What else could a fellow do
When Jones and Smith kept at me, and a dozen others, too?
I borrowed clubs from Thompson and put on Webster's shoes.
They had been urging me so long I couldn't well refuse.
But now that I have tried it, I still say as I have said,
That any fool who plays that game is addled in the head.

As we started off on number one, I saw a silly smile
On Jones's face. It made me mad. I'd hit that ball a mile.
So I picked out the heaviest club and swung with all my might;
But apparently I didn't swing that crazy club just right.
I missed that ball completely and fanned the atmosphere.
My better judgment told me, "You had better quite right here."

But whoever had sense enough when he was good and mad
To heed his better judgment. (Though we always wish we had.)
I played the entire eighteen holes. It took all afternoon.
I swung and missed; I dug the turf; I broke Bill Thompson's spoon.
I lost about a dozen balls; I put three in the lake;
I swung and swore; I swore and swung until my arms did ache.

I landed in each patch of rough; I was in every trap,
While all the while I cussed myself for being such a sap
As to ever touch a golf club, or let a so-called friend
Tempt me into such a nightmare; but I kept on to the end.
Well at last we finished and counted up the score;
Found I'd made the eighteen holes in a-hundred-eighty-four.

I went home tired and dirty, and as ugly as a bear.
I had a quarrel with my wife. I knew it wasn't fair
To blame her for my troubles with that idiotic game;
But, like many another golfer, I blamed her just the same.
I sat around all evening, hot, disgusted, tired and gruff.
It was awful; but thank heavens, I know when I've had enough.

So I'm telling you now, neighbor, if my friend you want to be,
Talk of other things, but never, *never* mention golf to me.
*I hate it!* But I've got to go out and play once more
Just to prove I can do better than a-hundred-eighty-four.

THROUGH THE YEARS

**1936**

Golf? Why yes! I play a little. Oh, maybe twice a week.
You see my work keeps me inside; and I really have to seek.
Some exercise and sunshine or I put on too much weight.
Then besides our course is beautiful; and I've noticed, too, of late
That out there one makes contact with some influential men.
A fellow needs such contacts in his business now and then.

But really, about the game itself, I'm not so very keen.
Of course I do enjoy it, but—well, you know what I mean.
I'm not one of those fellows who would rather play than eat,
Who will play the hottest noon hour and forget about the heat;
To whom home and business aren't important any more,
If only on the golf-course they can make a better score.

Now with me it doesn't matter if my score is low or high.
I get the same amount of exercise; and I don't really try
To become an expert golfer. No such is not my aim.
It is not the score that matters; It's the playing of the game.
Well, yes, I do take lessons. Took one the other night
If a fellow's going to make the game, he might as well play right.

**1940**

Say, Jones, you should have seen me on my third round yesterday.
You'd have thought I was Hagen if you could have watched me play.
A birdie on the second hole, and another on sixteen.
I was burning up the fairways; I was deadly on the green.
And back on number seven, I'd had an eagle, but
The caddy made me nervous, and I missed a two-foot putt.

I finished up that blistering round in three strokes under par.
The pro was playing with me, and he said it was by far
The best round he has seen this year. He thinks I ought to go
To Cleveland for the Open: says that I could steal the show.
I think myself that I could make their best look like a dub;
And I really should do something for the honor of our Club.

What's that? How is business? Well really I don't know.
You see, I've been so busy here that I've not had time to go
Down to the office for a spell. The family: They're all right.
At least I presume they are. I saw them Thursday night.
If I'm going to go to Cleveland, I can't neglect my game;
And business and the family will get along the same
Without me as when I am there. A telegram for me?
Oh hang the useless bother! What's in it? Let me see.
AM SICK AND TIRED OF LIVING A GOLF WIDOW'S EMPTY LIFE.
ELOPING WITH THE CHAUFFEUR. YOUR LONG NEGLECTED WIFE.

## *OPPORTUNITY KNOCKS BUT ONCE*

On Noah's ark there did embark,
    Because of rainy weather,
From west to east of every beast
    A pa and ma together.

The elephants both brought their trunks;
    The timid mice were wondery;
The crocodiles their famous smiles
    Bestowed on all and sundry.

The fauna all, both big and small,
    Filled ark from floor to ceiling.
And Missus No said, "Papa go
    And stop that awful squealing."

But one mistake did Noah make.
    His fame would be complete-o
Did he but try to swat the fly,
    And ditto, the mosquito.

## *TRAGEDY AT THE ZOO*

Said an animal-trainer named Lou,
Who worked for a Kalamazoo zoo,
When a nasty old shrew
Bit the zoo's gnu in two,
"That a shrew
        should not do
                to our gnu."

## ANOPHELES QUADRIMACULATUS

Life for me would be far sweeter
Were it not for the mosqueeter.

Alas! How often I have spent
Nights that were for romance meant,
When the moon shone bright above,
And the breezes whispered love;
But love and romance were forgot.
All we did was sit and swat.

Scientists seem to agree
That of mosquitoes, it's the she
Who does all the dirty work.
Not that hubby wants to shirk;
But he hasn't any tools,
So he sits around and drools
While the ladies have their tea,
With the menu mostly me.
Male mosquitoes then are good,
But the gals are out for blood.

If we can believe this tale,
Then I never saw a male.
All the skeets I ever see
Take a large-size chunk of me.
All the skeets in this fair land
Use me for a hot-dog stand.

If one mosquito is nearby,
To my room she's sure to fly.
Then, for sleep, I lose all zest
As I hear the buzzing pest
Droning o'er my bed at night.
I lie and wonder where she'll light.
On my neck or on my knee

Will that fiery itching be?
I swat—But swat the empty air;
The buzzing beast is never there.

I try to hide beneath the sheet;
She enters even that retreat.
She hums a while around my ear,
Then, cowardly, jabs me in the rear.
I scratch, but scratching makes it worse.
(Kind Lord, forgive me for that curse.)
So, through the sweltering summer night,
I wage a game, but losing fight;
And when dawn tints the eastern skies,
Full to the brim she homeward flies,
And asks her ilk from west and east
To join her in the next night's feast.

Yes, life would be a lot more fun
If, of mosquitoes, there were none.

## A SONG OF TWO SEA-GULLS

A sea-gull and his she-gull
    Went out one day to dine.
Said the greedy, grasping he-gull,
    "First fish we find is mine."

But the she-gull preened her feathers
    And gave her head a toss.
"You had better mind your manners
    And find out who is boss.

"Of all the droopy dumb-bells
    You surely are the worst,
For Emmy Post says always
    That it should be 'LADIES FIRST'."

The he-gull waddled down the dock,
    And snarled at his fair mate,
"I wonder if you realize
    How much you're gaining weight.

"Now, the chicks down by the sandbar
    Are slender, light and free;
And a frowsy, fat old she-gull
    Has no sex appeal for me.

"So, if you would hold your hubby,
    You had better take this tip:
Keep a close watch on your waist line,
    And button up your lip."

Then the fire-works really started,
    While the angry screaming grew,
As each one called the other
    Every nasty name he knew.

All other gulls fed freely
    On fishes live and dead;
But these two foolish birds at sunset
    Went hungry home to bed.

Now the moral of this little tale—
    If moral there must be—
Is that gulls don't differ very much
    From folks like you and me.

## ADVICE TO A YOUNG MAN

My dear young friend, I would defend
    Your youth so pure and tender;
So let me show all that I know
    About the other gender.

Please listen twice to the advice,
    The best I ever gave you.
If followed when you choose your friend,
    It may from error save you.

Look for a gal who is a pal,
    Intelligent and modest,
Who doesn't vex with too much sex,
    Whose clothes are not the oddest.

Who doesn't smoke or tell a joke
    She wouldn't tell her mother,
Who likes to bake a pie or cake,
    Who treats you like a brother.

But scorn the one who thinks that fun
    Alone makes life worth living,
The silly miss who thinks a kiss
    She must be always giving.

Through the night 'tis her delight
    To boogy-woog or rumba;
Brains has she naught, to think a thought
    To her is dull and dumba.

So turn away from damsels gay
    Whose only thought is pleasure;
And look around until you've found
    A sweet domestic treasure.

If you'll forget the girls who pet,
    Far sounder will you slumber.
So go and tell all such farewell—
    And let me have their number.

## FREEDOM

Muse of Parnassus, make me some noise.
    Your cooperation I seek.
I would sing of the freedom a husband enjoys
    When his wife goes away for a week.

The dishes from breakfast are stacked in the sink,
    And ditto the dishes from dinner.
The fact I must eat my own cooking, I think,
    Is the reason I keep getting thinner.

Ah, cooking's an art at which long I have toiled,
    And in it take wondrous pride.
I know that an egg can be poached, scrambled or boiled
    But, in practice, it always is fried.

I know that a salad for luncheon is served,
    And that soup is the thing for cold weather;
But I find that the dishes are greatly conserved
    By cooking my food all together.

I can't understand why a gingham-clad cook
    Spends hours in preparing a meal
And has to look recipes up in a book,
    Or bothers potatoes to peel.

Now my cooking is free from such worry, for I
    Am rid of all tiresome routines;
And my simple way of preparing a meal
    Is to open a can of baked beans.

And at night I am free to go out on the town,
    To ramble and roam as I please;
But I seem to prefer to sit quietly down
    And stretch out in a chair at my ease.

Oh yes, I am free to paint the town red,
    Or some other bright living shade;
But I start to yawn at eight-thirty instead—
    And then find that the bed isn't made.

In my dreams I am tempted by feminine charm
    Displayed without drapes or adorning
But ere I succumb, *clang* goes the alarm,
    And I wake up to find it is morning.

And then, I can't find a clean pair of socks,
    And a button has come off my shirt.
The empty house echoes the creaks and the knocks,
    Till the emptiness makes my head hurt.

It's been only three days since the morning she went.
    Tomorrow will be one day more.
It's great to be free; but I'd give my last cent
    Just to see her come in through the door.

## WOMEN'S UPLIFT CLUB

The regular meeting of the Uplift Club,
Held Thursday evening, January Three.
Meeting called to order by the President.
The roll was called—two members absent.
(A wink and nod were here exchanged
    Among the knowing ones.)
Minutes of last meeting—
    Read! Approved as read!
Treasurer's report is also ordered filed.
Chairman of standing committees each report—
"Your Committee has been active." Nothing more.
Communications—
A letter from the State Grand President,
Praising the noble work the Club has done.
Under Old Business—
Some changes must be made
To bring the Constitution up to date.
New business?
Yes. The By-Laws must be changed.
(See Section three of Article sixteen.)
The proposed change must be read,
Discussed,
And ratified.
The hour grows late.
The motion is in order to adjourn.
Moved! Seconded! Carried!

The Uplift Club has served its fellow-men.
The meeting stands adjourned.

## *YUST A YOKE*

William was a bovine who might have been a bull;
But he hadn't any pedigree; He hadn't any pull.
So for the fate that soon befell, we hope you'll shed a tear.
One simple operation, and Willie was a steer.

Now, Willie is indifferent to the most alluring cow;
And when it comes to making love, poor Bill
    Just don't know how.
Such fate has ne'er befallen me. I hope it never will.
Poor William is a simple ox. That's why the yoke's on Bill.

## *THE FLY*

I very often wonder why
The Good Lord ever made a fly.
He had His reason, I suppose;
But what it was, Lord only knows.

PART 5

# HISTORY—
# AND THE WAR YEARS

## *WAR-TIME RATIONING*
### *or,*
## *WE'LL BE SEEING MORE OF YOU*

Not far from this spot lives a young patriot,
And it's time that her tale should be told
For this marvelous child, so modest and mild,
Is a wonder that all should behold

When she goes for a ride with her swain at her side,
Her loyalty none can surpass.
They never drive far, just park his old car,
And save on the tires and the gas.

And when sugar ration alarms the whole nation,
She doesn't waste sugar, you bet.
She just hints that candy would be rather dandy,
And eats all the sweets she can get.

And when Uncle Sam got into a jam,
So that leather was scarce, and said, "I
Do really fear that three pairs a year
Will be all of the shoes you can buy."

This maid patriotic with taste so exotic
That she knew neither reason or rule,
She her shoes and her hose and painted her toes,
And then came bare-footed to school.

There were red toes and blue, and yellow toes, too,
And they looked very chic, I suppose;
But what worries me is the sights we might see
If they ever start rationing clothes.

## WINGS IN THE SKY

Wings in the sky!
Tireless grey wings that swiftly southward fly;
The graceful "V" of wildfowls travelling high,
Sounding aloft their free and joyful cry.

Wings in the sky!
Wings high above the Indian-summer's peace.
Hearing their call, the playing children cease
Their games, and gaily shout, "Wild geese! Wild geese!"

Wings in the sky!
And, far below, watching their distant flight,
We stand exultant at the free wild sight,
Until their forms are lost in gathering night.

Wings in the sky!
Dark, vulture wings, that over Europe soar,
Against a heaven black with the clouds of war,
Their flying song, a deadly sullen roar.

Wings in the sky!
Wings high above a wasted, barren land,
Where crumbling walls like blackened sentries stand,
And view destruction, spread on every hand.

Wings in the sky!
And wretched children, terror in their eyes,
Rush for the shelter where scant safety lies;
While, left behind, another playmate dies.

Wings in the sky!
Casting their deadly droppings from on high,
While humble victims vainly wonder why,
And wish to God that only birds could fly.

## WILLIAM TUFFS

*In a quiet spot in northern Indiana called Bonnyville Cemetery, is the grave of a man named William Tuffs. This is his story.*

William Tuffs, born seventeen, forty-two,
Died eighteen, forty-nine.
How much of history within that line!
Not in his more than century of years
But in his deeds the measure of his life appears.

For he was one who on a fateful night,
In Boston harbor, boarded Britain's ship
And threw the hated tea into the bay.
And in the bitter conflict that ensued,
He fought and starved and marched with Washington;
Endured hunger and cold at Valley Forge;
Knew the discouragement of long retreats;
But steadfast still until the cause was won.

The war over, turning again to his plow,
He won each year new acres from the wild,
Carving out wealth where there had been but waste.

War came again—The War of Eighteen-twelve.
Three score and ten, the allotted years of man, were his;
Yet William Tuffs once more enlisted in the ranks
And fought throughout the battles of that war.

Again came peace. The aged man might well
Content himself to sit beside the fire
And talk about the days that had gone by;
To tell the great adventures he had known.

Not William Tuffs!
He sold the fertile acres he had cleared,
And once again became a pioneer.
Far in the trackless wilds he made his way;
And there alone for more than thirty years
Fought hand-to-hand the stubborn wilderness
Before he died,
Aged one-hundred and seven.

I like to think his life a symbol of America.

      \*    \*    \*

Some years ago, the slab that marked his grave
And told the story of his wonderous life
Was stolen from its base and carried far
To serve somebody as a souvenir.

I wonder if that deed is also a symbol of America.

## WAHBEMEME[*]

*At the intersection of U.S. 12 and U.S. 131 in southwestern Michigan there stands a large boulder. The ravages of time have effaced much of the inscription that was carved there more than sixty years ago; but one can still read one word, "Wahbameme." With some little poetic license, these verses tell the story commemorated by this boulder.*

Beside the mighty stream where Huron flows
To mingle with the waters of Lake Erie,
Amid the circling forest oaks that towered
Like sentinels against the starless sky,
Brightly there burned an Indian council fire.

Around the fire, some resting on the ground,
Some talking eagerly, some whispering low,
Were gathered braves and chiefs from all the lands
Touched by the waters of the inland seas.

At last the great Tecumseh rose to speak.
Chief of the chiefs was he, whose mighty power
Had drawn these tribes which long had fought each other
To meet together in a common cause.
He raised his hand; and when a sudden silence
Fell on the throng, slowly he thus addressed them.

"Six days journey toward the setting sun
Where roam the deer and graze the buffalo,
The lordly white-man now has set his foot,
Built his log wigwams, and with unstayed hands
Cut down our forests, while his cattle's feet
Trample the ground 'neath which our fathers lie.
His mighty bow that shoots the thunder's arrow
Destroys our game; and now his young men take
Our fairest maids as playthings for their lust.

---

[*] The original title of this poem was misspelled "Wabameme." The name has been corrected throughout.

"You who have fought each other without fear,
Have laughed to feel the flying arrow's sting,
I call you now to meet this greater peril.
Let Ottawas, Ojibwas and the rest,
Forgetting tribal quarrels now unite
And drive the hated pale-face from our shores.

"Now they are few and our united braves
Can crush them like an egg shell in our hand.
They have no fear; they call the red man Friend.
They scatter far in forest and in field,
Taking no thought of danger, unprepared.
There in the quiet of the summer noon
Let strike the lightning of the red man's hate.
Like thunder let your war cries shake the earth.

"Their green corn fields will redden with their blood;
Your tomahawks shall still their children's cries;
Your hands shall choke the screams in women's throats.
And when the bloody scalps at last are counted,
Apply the torch that nothing may remain
To mark the place where stood the white man's cabin."

Fierce shouts that mingled bitter hate and joy—
Hate at the wrongs the chieftain's words had painted,
Joy at the thought of trophies to be won—
Greeted his words. The tom-tom's throbbing beat
Awoke weird echoes from the circling woods.
The dance of death began.
Like hideous monsters from some evil dream,
Circled the braves around the crackling fire.
The war paint glistened scarlet, yellow, green.
The war song, starting low like distant thunder
From a summer storm, rose shrill with hate
Until at last it seemed as if a wounded eagle screamed at bay.
The leaping, writhing dance still fiercer grew,
As if the fiends of hell had been turned loose
To frolic on the earth in holiday.

## THROUGH THE YEARS

One warrior only did not join the dance,
But stood apart among the flickering shadows;
And as the fierce, mad song of war grew wilder,
He stole alone into the forest gloom.
A youth he seemed, in age scarce twenty summers;
And yet he was a chief, Chief Wahbameme,
Chief of the Potawatomies upon whose soil
The pale face dwell whose death the council plotted.

The strong young face was clouded now with sorrow.
The Indians were his people; he was theirs.
But yonder in the cabins of the pale face
Lived one whom he called friend and brother too.
For one day as the Chief lay sick with small-pox,
Deserted by his tribe and all alone,
Feeling the hand of death was slowly closing
To snatch him to the land of spirit shades,
He saw a white man entering his wigwam.

The pale face saw the dread marks of contagion,
Saw too a man was dying there alone;
Forgot the danger of disease that threatened;
Thought only of a fellow man in need.
With gentle, skillful hands the pale face doctor
Drew back the red man from the grasp of death,
Brought food and drink and never left the wigwam
Until the Indian's strength had been restored.
And Wahbameme, listening to the war cry,
Seeing that fierce wild dance of savage hate,
Knew that against this friend the council plotted.

Then with a look of sudden stern decision,
Turning his back upon the council fire,
Silently he found the westward trail.
Then like an arrow speeding from the bow,
Sprang forward toward the land of setting sun.

All night he ran with steady, swinging stride,
Swimming the rivers, wading smaller streams.
The willow branches whipped against his face;
The berry briars scratched and tore his feet.

Night's darkness faded and the east grew pink;
But still he faltered not nor paused for rest.
Hour after hour those strong limbs bore him on;
Mile after mile the forest slipped behind.

High in the heavens now the midday sun
Beat down with cruel blazing torrid ray;
But Wahbeme sought no cooling forest shade,
Scarce stopped beside the spring to slack his thirst.
His limbs were aching now and bathed in sweat;
His heart was pounding, and his breath came fast.
He longed to stop beside some clear, cold stream
And for an hour his weary frame to rest.
But one hour's rest full well he knew might mean
Death for the one to whom his life he owed.

So through the long, hot summer afternoon he struggled on.
Sometimes he fell; but staggering rose again
And labored still along the westward trail.

The sun was sinking to the western hills
When Wahbeme reached the open prairie.
Before him lay the village of the pale face,
Peaceful, serene, without a thought of danger.
The shout of children, laughing in their play,
A song that floated through an open door,
The restful sounds that mark the eventide,
These scarce beat in upon his tired brain
As reeling, staggering, down the street he ran.
Two strong arms caught him as he stumbling fell.
Through dimming eyes he saw once more his friend.

Gasping for breath, the chieftain gave his warning,
"The red men come—to burn—to kill—to plunder.
My brother—it is finished—I am done."
His eyes grew dim; the tired form relaxed,
And Wahbameme slept among his fathers.

## *TO WAHBEMEME*
## *(a sequel)*

I wonder if you look, Oh Wahbameme,
Down from the hunting ground of spirits brave,
And see the injuries your people suffer,
The selfishness of those you died to save.

I wonder if you see the red man driven
Far from the hills and streams you used to roam
As exiles in a desert land of sage bush—
Rude huts of squalor there his only home.

I wonder if you see the white man's vices
Changing your people to a race of slaves—
Drunken, debased, dishonest, discontented,
The helpless victims of the pale faced knaves.

I wonder if you see the streams polluted
Beside whose waters clear you used to dwell,
The roaring, stinking, ugly tools of commerce
Making of lovely earth a piece of hell.

I wonder if you see the murdered bison
The vanished pigeon and the hunted deer;
Know that the hills that once were green with forest
Are gullied wastes, all desolate and drear.

And if you see and know, Chief Wahbememe,
I wonder if one thought comes swift and strong,
"The braves who danced around that council fire
Were in the right; and I was in the wrong."

## JUD SEPSEY*

I can see him yet as he played third-base
    There on the old ball field,
With always a smile on his sweating face
    And courage that would not yield.

We remember those games of basketball
    That were played on the old gym floor;
How he kept on trying and doing his best,
    No matter what the score.

He was called to play in a harder game
    Where there was no law nor rule;
But we know that he played there just the same
    As he played those games at school.

We know that his toil-worn face still smiled,
    Though the game was hard and long.
Though the playing field was a jungle wild,
    His courage still was strong.

Then the Great Coach saw he had done his part,
    Saw he had shown the stuff
That marks the man of heroic heart;
    So He said, "Well done. Enough!"

But the game goes on, and it must be won;
    And we are his teammates all.
We must fight the harder until 'tis done
    For the sake of those who fall.

---

\*   *Killed while fighting in the Owen-Stanley Mountains of New Guinea.*

## WAR MEMORIES

As I sit in the empty Assembly Room,
I seem to see in the gathering gloom
The boys who only the other day
Gathered their books and hurried away
With a roisterous shove and a boisterous shout
In the joy of knowing that school was out.

Remembering the time, not so long ago,
When Jim gave a paper-wad a throw
Just as I happened to enter the room.
I made him go and get a broom
And sweep the entire classroom floor,
So he wouldn't throw things any more.
Well, the paper-wads Jim's tossing now
Are hand grenades; and he should know how
To hit his mark with each one he throws.
He's had enough practice, goodness knows.

And then there was Tom. Remember him?
A whole lot quieter boy than Jim.
Sort of gentle and rather shy;
A kid who wouldn't hurt a fly.
But I read in the paper the other night
How during the Solomon Islands fight
Tom charged a blazing machine-gun nest;
Captured three Japs and killed the rest.

Remember Charlie? A regular pest!
One day while writing a Latin test
He made an airplane out of a sheet
Of note-book paper, and from his seat
Sent it sailing across the aisle
Where a fair haired girl with a sunny smile
Blushed as she saw two hearts entwine,
And knew that the plane was her valentine.
Charlie's flying a real airplane today,
In a land that is strange and far away;
And the valentines that he drops from high

Bring death and destruction from the sky,
While he looks down with a savage grin
On the flaming hell that was once Berlin.

And dozens of others; John and Jack;
Henry and George who will not come back;
Art and Harry and Fred and Bill;
And little Joe who could never sit still.
Some in khaki, and some in blue,
But each with a job that he has to do.
From polar cold to equator's heat
Echoes the sound of their marching feet;
And Children of future years shall read
Of each feat of arms and courageous deed.

But now as I sit alone in the room
And think of them here in the gathering gloom,
I ponder over again and again
How quickly boys turn into men.

## CONFLICT

He strikes me, so I hit him back
    And strike some harder blows.
His friends hit me; my friends hit them,
    And thus the conflict grows.

They call us names; we call them names.
    Like beasts they snap and snarl.
And so we too must snarl and snap
    As fiercer grows our quarrel.

Their hearts are full of bitter hate,
    So we hate in return.
As on our hate their hatred feeds,
    More bitter hate we learn.

They go to war; we go to war.
    To halt their cruel sway,
We teach our troops to be more cruel.
    They kill, so we must slay.

With lethal fumes they bomb our towns.
    The fiends! They shall not pass!
We build more planes; make larger bombs,
    And find a deadlier gas.

If tyrant foes conscript and draft,
    Conscript and draft must we.
And so, by crushing freedom,
    We seek to make men free.

We hate them for their foolish strife.
    Alas! We learn too late
That, hating them, we have become
    The very things we hate.

Then a Voice speaks from the ages,
    A humble voice and meek,
IF ANY MAN WOULD SMITE THEE
    TURN TO HIM THE OTHER CHEEK.

We have scorned Him as a weakling;
    We have said his Golden Rule
Was a silly dreamer's vision.
    We have mocked him as a fool.

But the great kings and their generals,
    With their battles, wars and strife,
Have not solved a single problem
    Nor enriched a single life.

And that calm Voice still is speaking,
    Like an echo from above.
"You can never know true living,
    Till you learn to live in love."

And at last we too are wondering,
    As we listen, Son of Man,
If those humble words of wisdom
    Might not be the better plan.

## *THE TIMES HAVE CHANGED*

The times have changed.
Two centuries ago, a plodding ox team drew a wooden plow
Amid the blackened stumps of new cleared land.
The hand-sown grain sprang from the virgin soil,
And harvest came.
With swinging cradle and with pounding flail, the pioneer
Won from the stubborn earth his daily bread.

The years pass by.
A single ox of steel dashes across the level even field,
Dragging behind a dozen plows that turn
More furrows in an hour than could a yoke
Of plodding oxen in a summer day.
The harrows follow and the wide-path drill;
And so by night the seed is in the ground.
The harvest comes.
And now the ox of steel draws mighty combines
Through the ripened grain.
One hour the wheat stands billowing in the wind;
The next the sacks of grain, all threshed and clean,
Start for the market in the near-by town.

The times have changed.
And yet today, on Twenty-second Street
I saw a child with pinched and hungry face
Crying for bread; but no one seemed to hear.

The times have changed.
Two centuries ago, along a forest trail that wound its way
Among the mighty oaks and towering pine,
Slowly a covered wagon rumbled on,
Now miring in the yielding swamp of clay,
Now jolting wildly over rocks and stones.
Day after day like snails they travelled on,
Those migrant souls who in the west would build
A mighty empire for their children's sons.

The years pass by.
The lonely forest trail becomes a road,
Smooth as a frozen pond and hard as stone.
The journey which the hardy pioneer
Could travel in a month of tedious hours,
His grandson, speeding like a winter gale,
Covers between the rising of the sun
And sunset of that self-same summer day.
Yet even so, above his head there wings
Another, traveling westward swifter still,
Who saw the morning sun from ocean rise
And shall tonight the broad Pacific see.

The times have changed.
And yet a week ago
I saw a traveler trudging by the pavement side.
Weary and worn he looked, and traveling far;
Yet no one stopped, and still he plodded on.

The times have changed.
Two centuries ago, beside the open hearth, the spinning wheel
Whirred at its endless task. The nearby loom
Yielded its homespun cloth for rich and poor.
The traveling cobbler with his simple tools
Wrought out by hand the sturdy boots and shoes
For the whole family. The furnishings of home
Showed still the marks of axe and hand-drawn knife.
The comforts that they had, such as they were,
Depended on their own strong arms and skill.

## THROUGH THE YEARS

The years pass by.
Beneath a factory roof a thousand wheels
Now spin a million threads, while neat at hand
A giant loom, driven by tamed lightning's force,
Swift as a hundred weavers, weaves each day
Oceans of cloth whose texture, rich and fine,
Shames the rude homespun that the fathers wore.
And yonder in those ugly piles of brick
A hundred swift machines that cut and sew
And paste and pound and grind,
Within an hour produce more boots and shoes
Than did the wandering cobbler in his seventy years.

The times have changed.
Yet only yesterday I saw a child
Walking bare-footed through the falling snow,
Ungloved and hatless, with a few torn rags
To shield his shivering body from the cold.

Yes, times have changed.
And yet sometimes as I survey the poverty of poor,
The wealth of rich; the roaring, whirling, maddening rush
    and roar
Of people striving for they know not what:
I go back home and sit alone and think,
And wonder is the change for good or ill.

## *THEY MARCH PAST SINGING*

They march past singing.
Strong young voices; strong young men:
Steady stride, heads erect, eyes straight ahead.
Every arm swings in unison—together;
And they sing.
They sing, even though they know that some will not return.
Even as they read the long lists of the missing,
They sing.

And you, America, are the theme of their song.
They sing of you, just as for you they will die—
Die singing. Oh America, be worthy of their song.

PART 6
# ROMANCE

## *FIRST LOVE*

Our love was like a garden
Where many flowers grow,
A bower of sweet profusion
With blossoms white as snow.

The hours we spent together,
Pure as an evening prayer;
The sparkle of you laughter,
The moonlight on your hair;
The quiet peace that filled me
Just to have you at my side;
The plans we made together,
Your look of joy and pride;
The tingling thrill that swept me
As your fingers brushed my hand;
The joy of sharing secrets
With one who could understand-
These were the flowers whose perfume
As they bloomed beside our way
Made our love like a garden
On a sunny summer day.

But to our lovely garden
We brought a wild rose red.
Its scarlet bloom was dazzling;
But the small white flowers are dead.

## *DUNGEON*

Life was a dreary dungeon cell
'Till your love opened wide the door,
And for the first time I beheld
The sparkling lake and distant shore.

I saw the mountains towering high,
And felt the breezes blowing free;
Saw silver clouds drift through the sky
Like white-sailed ships across the sea.

I felt the soft, warm voice as spring
Waking the earth from winter's sleep
I heard the song that thrushes sing,
Mating in woodland shadows deep.

   \*  \*  \*

The jailor's hand reclosed the door;
And now life's dreary dungeon walls
Enclose me tighter than before.
No gleam of hope in my cell falls.

## *PARALLEL LINES*

There is a tragedy in parallels,
Condemned be the postulate of Euclid never to meet.
See, side by side they stretch across the street,
Yet form no angle, never coincide.
Two other lines may meet to form a point
And raise a brood of angles all their own;
But not these two.
For though their span should reach a million miles,
Each goes its chaste, unswerving way alone.

But now another, who perhaps a fool,
Seems wiser far than Euclid to me,
Has said that parallels at last do meet
In some far place he calls infinity.

I like the thought—the two somewhere shall meet,
For are not they like to your life and mine—
Parallel, together yet apart.

## *CORN*

Yesterday
This field of corn
Was green and bright,
There was a frost last night;
And corn is black and dead
Today.

The sun
Again this noon
Shines bright and warm;
But stalks of frosted corn
Are not revived
By sun.

The frost
Need strike
But on a single night,
And corn is dead.
Love is like corn.

## *EVENING ON THE LAKE*

Lovers sit here in the twilight,
    While over the waters it seems
The moon paves a pathway of silver
    That leads to the land of their dreams.

## *SNOW*

Yesterday the world was sodden gray,
    A world of muddy gardens, naked trees,
    With naught of beauty that their eye might please
A desolate, dreary world—a dreary day.

But sometimes in the stillness of the night
    The miracle of freshly fallen snow
    Transformed the drab world in an hour or so
Into a world of beauty and delight.

The muddy garden glistens like a jewel
    Earth is a queen with diamonds in her hair.
    Trees, shrubs and fences robes of ermine wear,
Fit subjects for the glamorous queen to rule.

Tis true the jewels and ermine melt away.
    In deeper mud, more wretched than before
    The garden will be ugly mire once more.
But what of that, Earth is a queen today.

So from my life, your love must fade I know;
But for today, I have the fresh white snow.

## *JEALOUSY*

I did not sleep last night. How could I sleep,
When every time my eyelids closed I saw your face
And that fair form that I have often held
So fondly and so close in love's embrace?
Two months ago such visions brought me peace,
And lured to sleep and dreams of perfect bliss;
But not last night.

For now whenever I behold your face,
I always see another by your side.
Another's arms your slender form enfold;
Another's lips against your warm lips press;
Another's hand…! Another! Oh, my God,
Remove such thoughts before they drive me mad.

You showed me heaven; I tasted heaven's joy
But now the gates of heaven are closed to me,
And to another has been given the key.
Outside heaven's gate each night henceforth shall be,
As last night was, a night of hell for me.

## *TIMID LOVER*

I am afraid; and yet I do not fear
The many things of which men live in dread.
I have faced dangers, death, without dismay;
Walked untrembling through the unknown dark,
Where hidden dangers grasp from every side;
Walked without fear. and yet I am afraid.

I know that men walk daily as they do
Because they fear the scorn of fellow men;
That each is molded by the secret dread
Of retribution if he breaks the tribe's taboo.
I swear that no such fear restrains me now
From my desires. And yet I am afraid.

I know full well how strong, too, is the fear
Of angry fury from an outraged God;
How men have lived as slaves a thousand years
Rather than risk the breaking of some rule
Which they believed to be divine command.
I have thrown off such chains. And yet I am afraid.

And yet I am afraid. Afraid of what?
Afraid of you, dear one. Afraid the gifts you give,
The quiet talk, the hour together as the daylight fades,
Would be withdrawn should I dare ask for more.

THROUGH THE YEARS

## SILVER WEDDING

Twenty-five years ago tonight,
    Twenty-five years ago, dear.
Short were the years and swift their flight
    As we watched them come and go, dear.

Twenty-five years, can it really be
    Since that night when we were wed, dear;
When it seemed that angels smiled on me
    As those simple vows were said, dear.

Twenty-five years, and children came.
    Then yours was the tender hand, dear,
That cooled their brows from fever's flame;
    And 'twas you did understand, dear.

Twenty-five years, and as they grew,
    It was your task to guide, dear.
For every need that childhood knew'
    Somehow you could provide, dear.

Twenty-five years, and few indeed
    Were the dollars you had to spend, dear.
But in those lives you sowed the seed
    Of wealth that has no end, dear.

Twenty-five years and the children grown
    Are no longer by our side, dear;
But now, as we sit by the hearth alone,
    Our hearts glow warm with pride, dear.

Twenty-five years, and the graceful flower
    That I plucked that August night, dear,
Has sweeter grown with each passing hour.
    Its beauty still is bright, dear.

Twenty-five years, and my hair is gray,
    And my waist no longer slender;
But the smiles you greet me with each day
    Are loyal still, and tender.

Twenty-five years have brought grief and pain;
    And we have had our share, dear.
But like the sunshine after rain,
    There was a joy for every care, dear.

Twenty-five years, and I thank the Lord
    For you whom I adore, dear.
Nor would I ask more rich reward[*]
    Than twenty-five years more, dear.

---

[*] *The writer and his wife are thankful that we have been granted that "rich reward" of twenty-five years more.* [Written in 1968.]

## KINDS OF LOVE

Like one who, from afar,
Worships some god upon Olympus high—
Remote, untouched, and unattainable—
I worshiped you
In days that are gone by.

Or like one who, with cold appraising eye,
Admires the beauty of each curve and line
Of marble statue carved by Angello;
So I admired
In days of long ago.

But now the far-off god is human flesh;
And through the statue's snow white limbs I find
Flows blood as warm and red as flows in mine,
I worship still, and still I do admire,
But worship, admiration touched with fire.

## *HOPELESS LOVER*

I may find fame, but what is fame to me,
    For without you, I'd find it incomplete.
    If shared with thee, the laurel leaf were sweet;
But fate ordains that this can never be.

I may win fortune—gold and precious stone
    May give me all the power that wealth can bring.
    Alas! Such wealth would have a bitter sting.
I can not lavish it on thee alone.

The palace I might build, a prison cell
    Tho filled with every comfort king has known.
    The softest couch became a bed of stone,
For in my palace you will never dwell.

I have known kisses warm with desire,
    Yet on my lips their impress has been cold.
    The fairest maid were but a strumpet old.
Thy lips alone can kindle me to fire.

I have felt soft, warm arms my neck entwine,
    With all the hot, compelling lure of youth.
    To me but serpent coils they were in truth;
I want to feel no other arms but thine.

So life goes on—vain, empty, without thee,
    Barren as polar ice or desert,
    A hopeless wandering in a fruitless land.
That which I most desire can never be.

## GENERATION GAP

I wonder if we ever were
    As silly as that couple over there.
Look at him now, his arm around her waist.
    See the poor idiot gently stroke her hair.

You'd think a five-foot bench were room enough
    Without her sitting on the fellow's lap.
See that love-sick expression on his face;
    Lord pity such a silly senseless sap.

Look at them now, her head upon his breast!
    It's sickening the way their arms entwine.
Why don't their parents put a stop to it?
    I'd use a strap if they were kids of mine.

And they don't seem to care who watches them.
    What's the world coming to I'd like to know.
The wife beside him smiled and softly sighed,
    "That's you and I just thirty years ago."

The Robert Benjamin family, including Bob, Susan Margaret (Maggie), Stanley George (Stan), Gladys, and Bruce Phillips, and their dog Tallulah (Tutu), ca. 1962.

A 1958 Christmas card photo of the Edward Benjamin family, from left to right, George Wesley, Barbara Jane (Barb), Scott Frederick, Edward Leroy (Ed), Richard John (Ben), and their dog, Popper.

[TOP] This is the only known photo that includes all of the Holmes children together, but unfortunately didn't include Dorothy or Herbert. (Back row) Mark William, Cassandra (Cassie) Jane, Lucinda (Cindy) Jean, Amanda (Mandy) Jo and Jennifer (Jenny) Ruth, (front row) Molly Barbara, Justin Bruce and Heidi Carol, 1962.

[BOTTOM] Dorothy and Herbert Holmes, with Amanda, Heidi, Jennifer, Mark, Cassandra and Molly, ca. 1973. Not pictured: Cindy and Justin.

The Cade family (back row) Claudia Jane, Richard (Dick) Luke, Rebecca (Becki) Louise, and their exchange student, Rita Gupta Agrawal; (front row) Rena Lois, Norma Lillian and Martin (Marty) Marshal, mid-1960s.

The Knudtzon family, photographed during a family gathering in Cheboygan, Michigan, ca. 1966. From left to right are Kenneth (Ken), Helen Ilda, Kendra Marie, Kim Johanne, and Kurt Langton.

The William Benjamin family, including William (Bill) Howard, Esther Ann, David Stanley and Paul William, early 1970s.

PART 7
# PEOPLE AND PLACES

## FATE RIDES THE EVENING MAIL

*(Sort of ballad or something. 5% fact; 95% fancy.)*

The five-fifteen was a half hour late,
And running at seventy-five
And she thundered around the Galesburg curve
Like some monstrous thing alive.

A dragon belching smoke and flames,
With one great eye aglow.
Her whistle shrieked in the gathering night
As she plunged through the drifting snow.

The smoke and steam half hid he train
As she pounded along the rail
When Charlie McGuire, the postal clerk,
Threw off the evening mail.

Oh Charlie McGuire, the postal clerk
Was a faithful man and true;
And always, until that fateful night,
The mail-pouch well he threw.

But the wind that swept the icy street
Was a fiend that no pity feels.
The shrieking gale the mail pouch blew
Beneath the grinding wheels.

Oh pity, then, the postal men,
Who in that bitter gale
Searched in the gathering darkness
For each tattered piece of mail.

And pity, too, the office crew
Who heedless of the weather,
Toiled through the darkness of the night
To fit the scraps together.

Sigh also for the office force
Who worked for Burgess Seed.
The scrambled mail which they received
Was torn and mixed, indeed.

And Bill McPhee from Kankakee,
Who had ordered Wonder Tomatoes,
Probably sore when he received
Ireland's Pride potatoes.

And Franklin Glass of Springfield, Mass.
Undoubtedly muttered "Bosh!"
When the lawn, seed he had ordered
Turned out to be hubbard squash.

But if my pen aspired to try
To tell all the confusion
Caused by that scrambled mail, this verse
Would never reach conclusion.

So let me tell of two young men
Whose lives were most affected
Because the aim of Charlie McGuire
Had not been quite perfected.

Reginald Ruth was a charming youth,
Handsome and debonair,
Who never forgot to brush his teeth
Or comb his wavy hair.

## THROUGH THE YEARS

He was ever faithful to his work
At Kresge nickel and dime;
He never quit till the clock struck five,
He was always there on time.

And on the night on which occurred
The beginning of this tale,
A letter addressed to Reginald
Was in the evening mail-

A letter from a city girl
Whom he had never seen:
"I believe you are the nephew
Of my good friend, Mary Green.

"I am going to come to Galesburg
To teach the second grade;
And, since I've never been there,
I am just a bit afraid.
Would it be too much to ask you
To meet me at the station.
So that you can recognize me
I will wear a red carnation."

The other man our tale concerns
Was Rambling Reggy Doyle,
Who had sampled almost everything
Excepting honest toil.

The members of the Ladies Aid
Were scandalized to hear
That Rambling Reggy sometimes drank
A glass or two of beer.

Yes, Reggie was a touch young thug
According to these ladies,
Between playing cards and cigarettes,
He was headed straight for hades.

They prophesied that some day
He would surely land in jail.
For him too there was a letter
In that fateful evening mail.

"Dear Rambling Reg," the note began,
"Though we've never chanced to meet,
I have heard from one who knows you
That you never get cold feet.

"We have need of such a fellow
And, as matters seem to stand,
Can pay him for an hour's work
About a half a grand."

Yes, there two important letters
Both arrived that fateful day
When the mail was torn and scattered
All along the right way.

Ah woe is me! And woe is you!
And woe is everyone!
The cruel tricks that Fate may play
Can never be undone.

For when at last the postal clerks
Had finished with their toil,
The letter meant for Reginald Ruth
Was sent to Reggy Doyle.

THROUGH THE YEARS

And the note for Rambling Reggy
Was pieced and patched and then
Delivered to the honest Reginald
At the Kresge five and ten.

   \*  \*  \*

The Irish heart of Reggy Doyle
Could not resist the plea
Of any female in distress,
So to the train went he.

He waited at the depot
For the writer of the note;
And when he saw her standing there,
A lump rose in his throat.

For she was fair as any flower
That in a garden grows,
From shining curls of golden hair
To tips of tiny toes.

Poor Reggy Doyle fell fast and hard
As falls a wind-torn oak.
His voice was hoarse and trembling
When finally he spoke.

"Guess you must be the girl," he said,
"Who knows Aunt Mary Green.
I'll gladly help you find your way,
And that I truly mean."

He took her to the boarding-house
Which was her destination;
And at the door she handed him
The faded red carnation.

His heart beat tunes against his ribs.
He asked her for a date.
And when she softly whispered, "Yes."
He knew that this was fate.

Soon under love's benignant spell,
Reg quit his wandering way.
He got a job and settled down
And began to save his pay.

Of course they soon were married;
And the last time that I heard
They had two little Doyletts
And were looking for the third.

\* \* \*

Now we must turn to Reginald Ruth
Who got the other letter.
He, too, was interested,
Though he should have known much better.

Perhaps 'twas curiosity,
Or maybe it was greed.
Or it may be, like most of us,
More money he did need.

What e're his motives may have been,
Whether worthy ones, or not,
He met the writer of the note
And was drawn into their plot.

At first they told him that their scheme
Was but a boyish prank.
Too late he learned they really planned
To rob The First State Bank.

## THROUGH THE YEARS

Now Reginald was not a thief—
He never planned it so,
But just this once—well half a grand
Looked like a lot of dough.

So when, one dark and stormy night,
The gang their game did play,
He was the driver of the car
Used for their get-away.

But Gum-shoe Ike, the village cop,
A man of quiet charm,
Had watched the whole proceedings
And now quickly spread alarm.

Within an hour the state police
Were hot upon their trail;
And ere the morn the criminals
Were all locked up in jail.

Poor Reginald, poor Reginald,
Now rued the whole transaction.
He heard the judge one morning say,
"Spend fifteen years in Jackson."

   *  *  *

Ah, woe is me! And woe is you!
And woe is everyone!
And Charlie McGuire, you postal clerk,
Look what you went and done!

## TO A GRAY HAIR

The other morning, when I went to shave,
    Among my locks, I found one hair of gray,
Just one gray hair when all the rest were brown,
    And yet to me that one hair seemed to say

"You're getting old, my boy, yes getting old;
    Your hand will tremble and your back soon bend.
Along life's road, you've traveled many a mile.
    Old boy, you're coming somewhere near the end."

With one quick jerk I pulled that gray hair out.
    "You little liar, you've no business there;
I am not old; I'm only in my prime.
    I'll not be old because of one gray hair.

    "You're here too soon. Why, only yesterday-
    Or so it seems—I was a little boy,
Roamed carefree through the woods, beside the stream;
    Swam in the lake—each moment filled with joy.

"No, I'm not old; I can't be old—not yet.
    There is too much to do still left undone,
Too much of fame to win and gold to gain;
    Too many things I've planned, not yet begun.

"I want to sail the seas to far-off lands,
    And scale the peak of snowclad mountain high-"
This morning, where that one gray hair had been,
    I pulled out two. The gray hairs do not lie.

## ALAS! ATLAS

*(A fable from the Greeks, for School Superintendents and other Important People.)*

This Atlas boy was quite a lad,
    According to the Greeks;
But maybe when they told him,
    Their tongues were in their cheeks.

It seems that Atlas had a job
    Which must have been intriguing,
Though I suspect it was at times
    A little bit fatiguing.

For when the kids of ancient Greece
This question asked their olders,
"What does the big world rest upon?"
They answered, "Atlas's shoulders."

Yes, Atlas carried quite a load-
The earth, to be specific.
I doubt not that he sometimes felt
The pressure was terrific.

And many a summer afternoon
No doubt he stood there wishing
That he could lay his burden down
And spend an hour in fishing.

But poor old Atlas knew full well
That no one else in Greece
Could lift the load from off his back
And let his labor cease.

Atlas! The years flew swiftly by,
And Atlas grew no stronger;
Until at last there came the day
He could bear the load no longer.

Although he did the best he could,
The world began to slip,
And all of the neighbors realized
Old At had lost his grip.

He waited there to hear the crash
That surely must ensue.
Deprived of his supporting back,
What could the poor world do?

He looked a trifle silly
As he stood waiting there,
While Gravity took up the load
His shoulders used to bear.

The world still spins among the spheres.
According to my neighbors,
Though Atlas has, for many years,
Been resting from his labors.

So when you read the flattering tales
The papers print about you,
Remember this; perhaps the world
Could spin along without you.

## INDEPENDENCE

He vowed that he would ever
On himself alone depend.
So he never asked a favor—
And he never found a friend.

## *TWO VIEWS OF LIFE*

### FLOW TIDE

The tide is at its flow; along the shore
A wave creeps higher than was reached before,
And then recedes, leaving a foamy line upon the sand.

But the receding wave upon the beach
Is not the ebb. Another wave shall reach
Still higher on the sand. Each wave recedes,
But still the tide flows in.

So is it with the surging sea of men.
Waves may recede; but there shall come again
A higher wave, and progress—flowing tide—
Shall never ebb.


### THE SONG OF THE BEATNIK

At the top of the hill is nothing;
And climbing the hill is pain.
So why waste one's strength in striving
When there is no goal to gain.

Life is an empty beer-can
Thrown out on the pile to rust.
The froth and foam have vanished,
And the dregs have turned to dust.

The flower of love has faded,
Like grass without a root;
And one whom we once thought lovely
Is a worn out prostitute.

## HOPE

Black velvet night enshrouds the barren land;
    Lonely and lost I wander in the gloom,
While all around the shadowy ruins stand
    Like spirits beckoning towards a waiting tomb.

There is no path to guide my faltering feet.
    I see no glimmer of a friendly light.
The flags of hope are trailing in defeat
    Before the crushing legions of the night.

The faint and musty odor of decay,
    Bourn by the lifeless breeze from fetid fen,
Fills my discouraged spirit with dismay.
    A night bird moans, is still, and moans again.

And then the somber curtains of the night
    Are parted for a moment, and I see
One lovely star shine sparkling, clear and bright
    As if to light the dismal world for me.

The curtains close. Again I hear from far
    The owl's weird cry; but my dismay has flown,
For I have seen beyond the clouds—a star,
    And I have felt that I am not alone.

The fresh dew laves my weary, wounded feet;
    The musty odor of decay is gone;
The perfume of the rose is soft and sweet,
    And in the east I see the glow of dawn.

## WHISTLE

When it appears that the world's all wrong,
    Whistle.
When you haven't the heart to sing a song,
    Whistle.
For if you whistle a cheery strain,
You'll find things looking bright again,
Like a burst of sunshine after rain.
    So whistle.

When you have to carry a heavy load,
    Whistle.
When life drives with sharp-pointed goad,
    Whistle.
When your house of cards comes tumbling down,
When you think you haven't a friend in town,
And your old face twists with an ugly frown,
    Just whistle.

When the night is dark and you're afraid,
    Whistle.
When the goblin lurks in each deep, dark shade,
    Whistle.
For the worst of ghosts in the ghost of fear,
And he can't stand a note of cheer,
So when the night is dark and drear,
    Just whistle.

And when you come to life's setting sun,
    Whistle.
When you know that the race is nearly run,
    Whistle.
Though the stormy clouds have been dull and gray,
The morrow will dawn with a brighter day.
The Master of Courage has shown the way,
    So whistle.

## ANTS

Why all the labor, fierce activity?
You struggle to survive your little day.
You gather food, you reproduce—and die.
You reproduce another generation
Like yourselves,
Who in turn
Will likewise toil—
And reproduce—
And die.

Kindness it is you are not given to see
The endless circles, the futility.
You are but ants.

And what but ants are we?

## *APRIL SNOW*

Snow in December is beautiful,
    But snow in April ain't.
December snow can make things glow
    Like a glistening coat of paint.

But snow in April is something else,
    For April snows we hate.
Just when we're keen to see things green.
    Our gardens have to wait.

Snow in December is fine for sport
    So the skier can do his tricks.
But it's golf we play in April and May
    And golf and snow don't mix.

And April snow, when at last it melts,
    Makes gooey April mud,
While farmers wail that fruit will fail
    If frost has nipped the bud.

So let's have snow in December
    But in April give us showers;
For all we know that April snow
    Is not what brings May flowers.

## SPINSTER'S SOLILOQUY

They call me a woman of virtue,
While she is a woman of shame.
Yet sometimes I silently wonder
Which of us deserves the vile name.

She wanted from life what I wanted.
But what she wanted, she took.
While I sat alone with my virtue
And I read about life from a book.

Afraid of desire's fierce compelling,
Afraid of life's laughter and tears.
She dared and is damned for her daring;
I feared and am praised for my fears.

## *I RACE THE YEARS*

There was a time when I outran the years,
And had to wait while they caught up with me,
Impatient at their dragging, leaden feet

But in the race Time caught his second wind.
Perhaps 'twas when
I held my first-born infant in my arms.

The swifter years snatched him from cradle
Long before 'twas time;
Taught him to walk, when I would still have pressed
His curly head against my empty breast.

The speeding, taunting years
Taught him to run;
Trained him to march;
Gave him a deadly gun,
Taught him to kill—
And yet to me he's still
A pink-cheeked, laughing boy in overalls.

O swift, cruel years, you win!
I can not hold the pace that you have set.

## SNOW AT NIGHT

The headlights of my car cut with their beam
A tunnel through the mountains of the night;
And from its arching roof, the snow flakes seem
To spring into the shaft of dazzling light.

Out of the dark that lies beyond our ken,
Uncounted millions rush like some mad game.
They swirl a moment in the light, and then
Are swallowed in the darkness whence they came.

A million flakes have disappeared, but still
The air is crowded with the jostling race.
Out of the nowhere coming, going where?
They go, but other millions take their place.

A million snow flakes disappear. What then!
The storm goes on. *Snow flakes are like men.*

## LITTLE JIM HORNER

*(With apologies to Jack.)*

Little Jim Horner
Also sat in a corner.
He too was eating plum pie.
He stuck in his thumb;
But out came no plum,
And Jimmie began to ask why.

"Now Jack got a plum
When he stuck in his thumb
And he said it was 'cause he'd been good.
But I've been good as could be
And the truth seems to me
If Jack got a plum then I should."

You must tell little Jim
When you're walking with him
That the world is just like a plum pie
And the bad boy's thumb
Often pulls out the plum.
Life Jim, we sometimes wonder why.

## *LINES TO A VERY RECENT FATHER*

The colleges of this fair land
    Confer on us degrees.
Some are M.A., and some B.S.,
    And some are Ph.D.s.

Far greater are the marks of fame
    That come to you today,
For you can write after your name
    I now am a PA.

Yes, Papa, we now offer you
    Sincere congratulations.
We hope you'll know just what to do
    When come precipitations.

Such crises you will surely face,
    And then you'll have your chance
To learn life's greatest lesson—
    How to change the baby's pants.

## *LIFE*

Our ship upon a strange and silent sea
Seems to move.
The land from which we sailed,
Receding, drops below the ocean's rim.

The waters gaily gurgle round the prow,
Then seem to slip in silence swiftly past
As we remain unmoving and unmoved.

Surprised one morn, we see the farther shore
Loom just ahead—a harbor light!
Our voyage over ere we realize
It has begun.

## *I WALK LIFE'S PATH*

I walk life's path.
For yet a little while,
I still shall walk;
And then will come the night.

The path has sometimes led
Through darkened vale,
And then has climbed,
By toilsome steps, up to the sunny hill.

But vale or hill,
I have enjoyed the path.
Though sometimes seen through tears,
The landscape still grows brighter as I walk.

I do not know
What paths tomorrow holds;
But if I could,
I'd gladly walk again this very road.

## *A SONG OF REVOLT*

I am a down-trodden American laborer.
I work seven hours a day, five days a week. The rest of my
    time is my own.
My wages for a week are more than the yearly earnings of
    a laborer in many parts of the world.
I drive my own automobile. My wife drives hers. I drive to
    work; she drives to shop. Week-ends we drive for pleasure—
    fifty, a hundred miles—sometimes more.
I am part owner of the company for which I work. I help
    decide its policies.
When I am sixty-five—or earlier, if I prefer—I will retire
    with a comfortable income for the rest of my life.
I own my own home, complete with bath room, and air
    conditioning.
My wife cooks, washes, irons and sews with electricity.
    Our electric icebox is always well stocked with the best
    of foods.
When we feel like it, we attend the movies or a concert.
    When we remain at home the best of music and entertainment
    is brought to our living-room by radio and television.
Parks, playground and million-dollar-schools are provided
    for my children.
My oldest son is attending college, studying law. He will
    go far in politics—a governor—a senator. Who knows?
My necessities, fifty years ago, would have been considered
    the most extravagant luxuries of the richest millionaire.

How long will the millions of downtrodden American laborers
    like me allow The Establishment to continue such
    exploitation?

## ANTICIPATION AND REALITY

I want to see a football game,
    When autumn morns are chill,
And frost has spilled his paint pots
    On the distant, misty hill.

I want to see the banners
    Floating high above the trees,
And feel the lingering summer
    In the warm October breeze.

I want to see the color gay
    That fill the circling stands,
And watch the swift gyrations
    Of the briskly marching bands.

I want to feel the silence
    That awaits the opening kick
In that one long breathless moment
    When pulse beats high and quick.

I want to hear the murmur,
    Swelling to a mighty roar
As our twisting, shifting halfback
    Plunges over for a score.

And when the game is over,
    And our victory has been won,
To drive home in the splendor
    Of the setting autumn sun.

And as the stars start twinkling
    While the light fades from the west,
We will have a happy feeling
    That life is at its best

\*   \*   \*

I went to see the football game.
It rained—a dismal drizzle all the afternoon.
And our team lost.
After the game, a traffic jam,
A dented fender, a punctured tire.
Then home at last.
For dinner, cold bean soup.

## FROM THE BLUE-WATER BRIDGE

*(Author's note: When the international bridge was being constructed between Port Huron, Michigan, and Sarnia, Ontario, it was my privilege to walk with a group of Sarnia Rotarians out onto the unfinished span (around 1938) to the international boundary, where we stood for a moment with one foot in Canada and the other in the United States. That moment was the inspiration for these verses.)*

We see familiar scenes spread there below;
Yet viewed from this new vantage point they seem
Strangely remote and new, an afterglow
Of places half-remembered from a dream.

There sparkling like a jewel, Lake Huron lies,
Her sky-blue waters meeting sea-blue skies,
Her beaches, gleaming white on either hand,
With laughing children playing on their sand,
Like silver ribbons curve away between
The green of water and the darker green
Of pine clad hills that stretch along the shore
Till, dimmed by distance, eye can see no more.

Beneath us flows the river's mighty tide
Seeking the ocean. On its bosom ride
Great ships of commerce with their loads of grain
Gathered from far-off, fertile western plain
To feed the hungry peoples of the world.
While smaller crafts with banners gay unfurled,
And snow-white liners, too, pass swiftly by,
Trailing their plumes of smoke across the sky.

On either side the stream a city stands.
How like they are, and yet in different lands!
Their customs, people, language are the same;
Their difference, but a difference in name
And in the flag that floats above their trees.
Old Glory here floats gaily in the breeze,
While there the Union Jack looks proudly down,
Proclaiming loyalty to Britain's crown.

Two different lands, and yet somehow we feel,
Two friends drawn closer by this span of steel.
And to these spanning girders here today
God's sunshine, stream on them, seems to say,
"Proclaim to all the world till time shall cease
Two nations here join hands and dwell in peace."

## DESERTED HOUSE

At the foot of the hill the pavement wide
Stretches away to the busy town;
And cars flow by like a flowing tide,
While an old house squats on the hill-top brown.

Like a battered crown on a shaggy head,
The old house sits on a briar-grown hill.
The fallen leaves on the ground lie dead,
And a cold rain beats on the rotting sill.

The muddy path that upward leads
From the rusty gate to the broken door
Is dankly overgrown with weeds.
Sagging and worn is the old porch floor.

Like empty eyes in a skell long dead,
The sashless windows' vacant stare
Fills with a melancholy dread
Him who might seek seclusion there.

And if he enters the moldering room,
The empty echoes creek and creep
Like ghostly footsteps through the gloom
That fills each corner with shadows deep.

Here in the parlor a dusty toy,
Hidden behind a forsaken chair,
Has waited long for the little boy
Whose careless hand once dropped it there.

This was the kitchen, where busy hands
Started their task before the dawn.
But the crumbling cupboard empty stands,
And seems to whisper, "They are gone."

Where are they now, with their joys and woes?
The north wind answers, "No one knows."
And the tall pines echo with a sign,
While the traffic hurries unheeding by.

## *COTTAGE IN WINTER*

"Welcome Inn."
But the door is locked,
And the path is drifted deep with snow.
The soft, warm lake with ice is blocked;
No sparks in the friendly fire-place glow,
But only ashes. I should not go
To the cottage in winter, for when I do
The empty chill where once was warmth
Reminds me too much of you.

## *SPRING*

Spring!
Spring in a subdivision.
No song of poet; no singing bird.

Mud!
Dirty gray snow—dirty gray earth—smoky gray sky.
Black pools of water on a black cinder road.
A car hub-deep in the mire.

Little gray houses, all badly in need of paint,
A garage door hanging crazily on one hinge.

Vacant lots, scraggly with last summer's weeds-
Gardens—mud—water—slush.
Rotten tomatoes clinging to withered vines.
Cabbage stumps, half covered with potato peelings,
And thrown out slop.

Empty tin cans everywhere
Skeleton of a discarded automobile.

Spring!
Spring in a subdivision.

There by an open sewer, I found a flower,
A violet.
Spring!

## *THE TEACHER*

In a fertile spot by the side of the road
    He planted a tiny seed.
It sprang to life; and as it grew,
    He battled each choking weed.

He trained the tiny, tender twig
    To grow as a twig should grow.
He sheltered it from summer sun
    And the crush of winter's snow.

The tiny twig became a shrub;
    The shrub became a tree.
Sturdy and strong was the towering trunk
    As only an oak can be.

Strong with a strength that was more than the strength
    Of him who had helped it grow.
For thus the reward shall ever be
    That the Sower-of-Seeds may know.

Uncle Bill Benjamin watches as Grandpa Stanley teaches Cindy Holmes the finer points of Tic-Tac-Toe in the early 1950s.

Grandpa Stanley's competitive spirit held sway even when playing games with his grandchildren. Here he plays checkers with Aunt Barbara Benjamin and Cindy Holmes, early 1950s.

Stanley Benjamin enjoyed all games of strategy, including word games. Here Bob, Maggie, Ben and Stan join him to play Scrabble.

[TOP] Heidi Holmes playing cribbage in 1970 with Grandpa Stanley, a game not hindered too much by her broken arm.

[BOTTOM] Grandma Lillian stays just outside of the fray of a Holmes family picnic in 1963.

PART 8
# RELIGION

## TWO PRAYERS

In the quiet hour at the close of day
Two men came up to God's house to pray.
Each knelt at the altar and bowed his head;
And this is the prayer that the first man said:

"O Lord, who from my weary soul
Didst cast out sin and make me whole,
Breathe on me with celestial fire.
Keep me from every wrong desire;
And grant that through eternity
I may find rest and peace with Thee."

He said, "Amen"; rose to his feet
And hurried out to the busy street,
Where he turned his gaze to the sunset sky,
Nor saw the crowds that were passing by.

When the second man was left alone,
He spoke in a simple, quiet tone,
As if in the hush of that holy place
He and his Lord met face to face:

"There is hunger, Lord, on every hand,
Hunger at home and in foreign land;
Hunger in Poland, hunger in Greece—
Starvation and hunger that never cease.
And even here, on this very street,
Are those with never enough to eat.
You fed the hungry in days gone by;
Give now the bread for which children cry.

"And out on the street is a crippled child,
I can't forget how brave he smiled,
Nor the cheery way that he said, 'Hello.'
The Christ, back there in the long-ago,
Healed the lame, gave sight to the blind,
Brought quiet and peace to the troubled mind.
Still use that healing power today
That again this lad might run and play.

"And yonder is one who bears the name
Of the crimson path and the way of shame.
No friendly hand to her is given;
She has no hope for earth or heaven.
The righteous turn their heads in scorn,
Nor care for the burdens she may have bourn.
With gentle forgiveness in days of yore,
The Christ told such, 'Go sin no more.'

"But crueler that hunger or social ban
Is the jealous hatred of man for man.
Evil for evil we must repay;
O Christ, could we but hear Thee say,
As the nails in thy hands tear through and through'
Forgive, for they know not what they do.'

"And, Lord, if these poor hands of mine,
So clumsy and crude compared to thine,
Can help the ones for whom I pray,
Then, Jesus of Nazareth, show me the way."

## *FAILURE*

*(A Good Friday Thought.)*

A Failure! Hanging in disgrace upon his tree
    While on the skull-shaped hill and all about
    Those we would heal in cruel derision shout,
And pity not his dying agony.

A Failure! Dying there between two thieves,
    Forsaken e'en by those he loved the best,
    Mocked, scorned and spit upon by all the rest.
Not for the nails, but for their scorn he grieves.

But see, the suffering face relaxes in content,
    And those who mock are struck with sudden fear
    As from his ashen lips strange words they hear,
"The work is finished for which I was sent."

The work is finished; and it matters non
    Whether a cross or crown be his reward.
    There is no failure if the task is done
That has been given to each man by his Lord.

    *John XIX, 30*
    *"It is finished."*

## *CREATION*

"Let there be light." Light was!
Divine command, no sooner uttered that it was obeyed.
Creation started; and from that first hour
The hand of the Creator has not stayed.

Not in the six little days that Power created
The wonderous planet which we call our earth.
And threw it spinning mid the constellation:
Not thus this sphere of ours was given birth.

But slowly, ever through the endless eons
That Power has breathed on twisted, molten rock.
His vaporous breath has wrought disintegration;
The granite crumbled at His earthquake shock.

And when at last the sphere for life was ready,
The Power did or himself to earth bestow,
A grain of dust became a living creature,
Able to feel, to reproduce, to grow.

Able to grow, and through uncounted ages
The spark of life passed on from cell to cell.
A million years to change from fish to reptile;
But what are years to one who buildeth well.

And so today that Power is still creating,
Changing to meet an ever-changing plan.
Through many forms, the spark of life transmitted,
Has reached the form which we today call MAN.

But think not yet Creation's work is finished:
Think not that man must be its noblest son.
What lies beyond, we know not; but we know
That Power's creative work is not yet done.

## SQUIRE BURGER

Squire Burger used to go to church
    As his father did before;
But no, not more than once a year,
    He ope's the temple door.

So one day, when it came just right
    And the question seemed in season,
I asked the good squire if he would
    Disclose to me in the reason.

The answer that this good man gave
    Has had such frequent use
I suspect it's not the reason,
    But an overworked excuse.

"Our church has a new preacher
    For whose style I do not care.
The groves were God's first temples,
    And I'd rather worship there.

"No lofty, towering steeple,
    However grand and fine,
Can awake by sense of reverence
    Like a heavenward pointing pine.

"And the sermons of the preacher,
    Though he be both good and wise,
Can never match the preaching
    Of the sunset-tinted skies.

"The pealing of the organ
    And the choir-chanted words
Never lift my soul toward heaven
    Like the singing of the birds.

"And that something so inspiring
    About cathedral's colored glass
Can not match the flickering shadows
Playing on the forest grass—"

The real reason why he worships thus
    The Squire did not relate:
In the temple of God's Great Outdoors,
    There's no collection plate.

## *SPRING MEDITATION*

I sat alone in church
And humbly bowed my head.
The preacher droned a prayer;
I don't know what he said.

Outside an open window
Perched a gaily singing bird.
I closed my eyes and wondered
Which God heard.

## LIFE'S CHALLENGE

Sometimes I long for life of quiet ease
On some warn isle, girded by coral strand,
With palm trees swaying in the scented breeze,
And untilled fruitage free to all the land.

To have no thought of 'duty'; to be free
From every binding chain of 'right' and 'wrong,'
To dream to drift on gentle rippling sea—
I wish for this, but do not wish it long.

Such wishes come when weary, sick with pain,
I seek my couch, tortured by black despair;
But with the morn I rise refreshed again,
And rather this shall be my morning prayer—

No! Let me face the bitter storms of life;
Let flash the lightning and the thunders roll.
I flinch not from the suffering and the strife,
For 'tis by struggle that man builds a soul.

Let come the conflict then, whate'er the odds;
Turn loose the demons from the darkest pit.
I may be bruised and beaten; by the gods,
I swear whatever comes, I will not quit.

Too short life's day to ask for peace and rest;
Too soon shall come the quiet peace of death.
So to the fray! However goes the quest,
I will fight on as long as I have breath.

## *A PRAYER*

Lord, give me open eyes that I may see
In every dawning day a different light
Than crimsoned other dawns; and let me hear
New thrilling notes of joy in robin's song,
Though song and singer may be still the same
That woke the world from slumber yesterday.

## *EASTER*

Easter!
Church bells clang.
Along the avenue that peafowls strut
Parading their new spring feathers.

Easter!
Within a vaulted room
A preacher drones
Something about a 'resurrection,'
And an empty tomb.

Easter!
A stuffy matron whispers to her spouse
About the sermon—
Or her neighbor's hat.

Easter!
The banker nods his head,
Perhaps agreeing with the holy words,
Perhaps drowsy from last night's poker game.

Easter! A week ago this hill was brown and dead.
Today I found an arbutus.

## NOT MY HANDS

*(Based on the story of a member of Eddie Rickenbacker's crew.)*

We drifted alone on an empty sea
    With never a ship in sight.
The sun was cruel with its noon-day heat,
    But the air stung cold at night.

For days in our boat we had drifted thus,
    Since the peril of that fateful hour
When the lurking death of the submarine
    Struck with its lightning power.

There had come a day when our food ran low,
    And hunger's boney hand
Wrang all the strength from our withered limbs
    Till we could scarcely stand.

Then we prayed for food; and as we prayed
    On that boundless sea afloat,
A fish leaped high from the ocean's depth
    And landed in our boat.

We ate the flesh, quivering flesh,
    Till there was no more to eat;
We drank the blood, the red, red blood,
    And God but it tasted sweet.

But after that our casks ran dry;
    And the waves which seemed kind at first,
Mocked with their cruel, salty spray
    The pangs of our burning thirst.

Like the shimmering heat from molten iron
    Was the scorching sun's cruel ray.
Our parching lips could scarcely speak
    Our words as we tried to pray.

Then appeared a cloud in the western sky.
    We could see the falling rain;
But the wind was blowing the storm away,
    And it seemed that our prayers were vain.

Once more we prayed—that the wind might change;
    Aye, we prayed on bended knee.
The wind blew harder, and round our boat
    Seemed to laugh with a fiendish glee.

And then, as if pushed by the unseen hand
Of One who ruleth all,
The storm moved back against the wind,
    And the rain began to fall.

As if the skies were opened wide.
    The cooling torrents fell.
We slacked our cruel, burning thirst;
    And we filled our cask as well.

But still the dreary days dragged on;
    And again we weaker grew,
Till only I had the strength to stand
    Of all our stricken crew.

And then it was, when hope had fled,
    That I saw at last the land;
Green palm trees swaying in the breeze
    And the white of wave-washed sand.

But the tide was strong and the waves ran high,
    And they drove us from the shore.
I grasped the oars and tried to row
    As men never tried before.

Against that pull of wind and tide
    The arms of a dozen men
Could not have driven our drifting craft;
    But I tried, and tried again.

My strength was spent; my arms were weak;
    I could scarcely lift an oar.
Then our boat turned swiftly; and like a launch,
    It sped toward the waiting shore.

There were lands on those oars that were not my hands;
    There was strength that was more than mine.
The hands on the oars were the hands of God,
    And the strength was a strength Divine.

We landed safe—alive and safe—
    And we found the homes of men,
Ah, but 'twas good to feel the earth
    Beneath our feet again.

But out of those weeks one thing I learned:
    I know that come what may,
There are Other Hands, more strong than mine,
    To help me along my way.

## *A WISH AND A PRAYER*

May you reach each star toward which your feet are led;
Then may you see a brighter star ahead.

## THERE WERE TEN:
## A STORY FOR THANKSGIVING

*(See Luke's Gospel Chapter XVII; verse 12 to 19.)*

There were ten who sat by the dusty road
    Where the sun beat down from an oven sky,
Broken and bent by life's heavy load—
    Ten lepers waiting there to die.
Poor, wretched, forsaken by every friend;
    Forbidden to pass through the city gate;
Doomed by disease to a loathsome end,
    With nothing to do but sit and wait.

There were ten, ten creatures who once were men.
    More pitiful sight was never seen.
As they hoarsely croaked to each passerby
    Again and again, "Unclean! Unclean!"
Begging for crumbs that they might find
    Strength to endure another day;
Though death itself was far more kind
    Than the living death of such as they.

There was ten who saw as morning came
    The form of One they had longed to see,
For they had heard how he healed the lame
    And gave sight to the blind by Galilee.
And as they saw him from afar,
    They lifted their voices with one accord;
"Oh blessed Son of David's Star,
    Jesus, Master—Have mercy, Lord."

There were ten who heard that gentle voice,
    "Go show yourselves to your village priest,
For those who scorned you will rejoice
    And set before you a welcoming feast."
They limped away in the rising morn,
    And as they traveled the rocky ground,
Amid the tangle of briar and thorn
    Their flesh grew firm, and their limbs waxed sound.

There were ten—ten leaping, laughing men,
    With joy in the strength of once withered limb—
But only one who turned back again
    To utter one word of thanks to Him.
There were nine who never a hand did lift
    In thanks for the Love that lasts forever:
Too overjoyed by the matchless gift
    To return and thank the matchless Giver.

There were tens of thousands who yesterday
    Were touched by the Master's forgiving hand,
Then hurried unheeding along their way
    Because they did not understand
That this was the gift of the Master's grace
    Purchased for them upon the road.
Oh Christ, remove from before they face
    The sin of our base ingratitude.

## *LIFE VALUES*

It matters not that I may never know
Wealth and the honors that on fame depend,
If I can look when coming to life's end,
With satisfaction back along the road;
And see where I have lightened someone's load.
If so, the evening skies above shall glow
With promise of tomorrow, while below
The evening will be filled with joy and light.

But though I may find wealth beyond dreams;
Though fame and honor shall alike be mine,
If busy in their quest I shall decline
To listen to a comrade's burdened tale,
Or hearing it, and able, I shall fail
To share his burden; then to me it seems
The sunset will have lost all golden gleams,
And evening will be but the fall of night.

## TO MYSELF AT 70

The snows of seventy winters crown your brow.
The frosts of seventy autumns chill your veins,
Yet be not one who at the years complains,
Who mourns their passing and forgets their gains.

True, youth is springtime, smiling, laughing Spring,
When hopes mount high like eagles on the wing
And hearts beat time to songs the bluebirds sing.
Yes, youth is April, with her sudden shower
Turning to laughing sunshine in an hour,
Eager to pluck each quickly-fading flower.

But he who things that Spring alone has flowers
Knows not the glory of the Autumn hours,
When gentians bloom among the tall marsh grases,
And Summer lingers as October passes.

Here is a peace that Spring can never give,
When—harvest gathered—we find time to live;
To rest an hour beside an open door,
And grasp the beauty that we missed before.

We see ahead the hill where maples blaze,
Their outline dimmed by Indian-summer's haze;
And know that just beyond that shrouded hill
There is another valley—fairer still.

## NEW YEARS AUDIT

He sits in his office with furrowed brow,
    As the old year draws to its final close.
He adds and subtracts to determine how
    Much greater his assets than what he owes.

Outside the window the whirling snow
    Drifts by unheeded. His head is bent
Over his ledgers, determined to know
    How much his income, and how much he spent

The columns of figures are dimly seen,
    As the shadows closer about his press;
To him their totals alone will mean
    A year of failures or success.

Perhaps he dozed as the light grew dim
    And the lamps in the street began to shine,
For it seemed that a soft voice spoke to him:
    "Would you measure your life with a dollar sign?

"Are dollars and cents the only gain
    To show for the year that nears its end?
For this did you suffer toil and pain,
    To earn more money than you could spend?

"Turn again to your balance sheet,
    And enter another item or two
To make your reckoning complete,
    And make your inventory true.

"What of those sunny summer hours
    When you wandered beside a sparkling stream,
Where the air was perfumed by blossoming flowers;
    And you had only to fish and dream?

"And what of that bright October day,
    When frost had painted the northern woods,
And the flaming maples seemed to say:
    Behold, the Maker of All is good.

"Remember again another day,
    When you paused to comfort a weeping child:
How, as you wiped his tears away,
    He clung to your clumsy hand and smiled.

"Enter such items, great and small;
    And closing your ledger, you may find
That these are the greatest gains of all—
    A God more real, a heart more kind."

## MY NEIGHBOR

Although he walks with quiet, cat-like tread,
My neighbor's footfalls fill out street with dread.
He walks at night—alone—while others sleep,
His step as silent as the shadows deep
That lurk around the door of his abode.
That house, sequestered from our busy road,
Stands in a grove of dark and murmuring pines;
And from its shuttered windows no light shines.

And when my neighbor stalks along our street,
We scurry home on panic-driven feet,
Like sheep when prowling wolves attack at night.
We hurry home and turn on every light,
As if our man-made dawn would bar his way.
We bolt the door, thus hoping to delay
His entrance, though well we know that locks
Can not secure the door which he knocks.

One winter night when freezing, driven rain
Drummed drearily against my window pane,
And winds moaned low in treetops overhead,
My neighbor came, and stood beside my bed.
We had supposed his voice was harsh and cruel;
But when he spoke it was like waters cool
That ripples over rocks of some clear stream,
Or music from some half-forgotten dream.

He drew work pictures of the sunset sky;
Of billowing mists that cloak the mountain high;
Of sparkling lakes, wave-dimpled by the breeze;
The scent of blossoms in gnarled apple trees,
He spoke of wild geese in their southward flight;
The haunted stillness of the desert night.
He told the beauty that the seasons bring—
Lush meadows, verdant in their garb of spring;
Summer, with her fields of ripening grain;
Autumn, painted over hill and plain;
Winter, with her white, new-fallen snow
Blanketing the life that sleeps below.

And then he paused: "If men could only see,
I am a part of these, and these of me.:
And as he turned and left me for a while,
His dread face seemed to wear a kindly smile.

## CITY OF SAND

I built a city, a city of sand
    By the side of the silent sea,
A city with walls and castles grand
As were ever built by the busy hand
    Of a little child like me.

Of sticks and stones were the people made
    In my city by the sea;
And none was unhappy, and none afraid,
For each man worked at a noble trade,
    And every man was free.

The streets were paved with shining shell,
    In my city by the sea;
And from a steeple a tiny bell
Rang in the breeze as if to tell
    Of a better time to be.

Next morning I hurried on eager feet
    To my playground by the sea,
Planning my city to make complete
With trees and grass and flowers sweet;
    And I laughed with childish glee.

But during the night my city grand
    Had vanished without a trace,
For walls and castles made of sand
The white-capped waves could not withstand;
    And nothing marked their place.

    \*    \*    \*

Is the life God gives a city of sand
    That shall but for an hour abide?
Are we but playthings in his hand,
Built for an hour on a sunny strand,
    Then carelessly cast aside?

Will nothing remain to mark our place,
    When the city shall cease to be?
Is this the end of the human race?
Is blind oblivion all we face,
By the shore of time's empty sea?

    \*    \*    \*

Hark! A voice that speaks from an empty tomb
Each year shall assurance give:
Be not dismayed by death's seeming doom;
Light shines amid the deepest gloom.
Christ lives, and we shall live.

Aye, The house He builds is not of sand,
    But made of stuff sublime.
Somehow our spirits understand
By faith we may grasp the Builder's hand
    And march on through unending time.

## ANOTHER VALLEY

I wonder if beyond those far green hills
Whose mist-dimmed heights this vale of our enclose,
There is another valley like our own,
Where summer breezes, perfumed by the rose,
Blow soft o'er meadows green, and bring repose
To travelers weary from the toilsome road.

I wonder if the friends who said good bye,
And left this valley by that upward road
Have found beyond the hills a new abode,
And there laid down the traveler's weary load
To rest in sunshine of summer day.

And as I journey toward that mountain high
That marks so soon our valley's farthest end,
In the still air, it sometimes seems that I
Can hear afar the brave voice of a friend,
And see, as soft the evening shades descend
Above the hills a friendly guiding light.

The grandchildren of Stanley and Lillian Benjamin, ca. 1966, on the steps of the Congregational Church, Cheboygan, Michigan. Back row: Mark Holmes, Jenny Holmes, Kim Knudtzon, Cassie Holmes, Claudia Cade, Cindy Holmes, George Benjamin. Middle row: Stan Benjamin, Kurt Knudtzon, Amanda Holmes, Scott Benjamin, Molly Holmes, Heidi Holmes. Front row: Bruce Benjamin, Kerry Knudtzon, Kendra Knudtzon, Rena Cade, Maggie Benjamin, Becki Cade (holding Martin Cade), and Richard (Ben) Benjamin. Of all of the grandchildren, the only ones not pictured are Justin Holmes, who was away at summer camp, and David and Paul Benjamin, who weren't yet born.

The legacy of Stanley and Lillian Benjamin was evident at this 12 July 1999 Benjamin family reunion in Wisconsin that included great-grandchildren, but not yet great-great grandchildren.

The grandchildren of Stanley and Lillian Benjamin in 1978 at their 60th wedding anniversary. *Back row:* Becki Cade, Kim Knudtzon, Kendra Knudtzon, Kurt Knudtzon, Jennifer Holmes, Claudia Cade, Lillian Benjamin, Stanley Benjamin, Marty VanKirk. *Front row:* Martin Cade, Molly Holmes, Amanda Holmes, Kerry Knudtzon, Cindy Holmes, David Benjamin, Paul Benjamin. Not pictured are Cassie, Mark, Justin and Heidi Holmes, Rena Cade, and Bruce Benjamin.

Grandpa William offering turkey—in honor of all the family gatherings where food, memories, and passing on of family lore helped define the next generation through thick and thin.

At the farm in Springvale, Michigan.

www.ingramcontent.com/pod-product-compliance
Lightning Source LLC
Chambersburg PA
CBHW051353110526
44592CB00024B/2975